STRENGTH BEYOND MEASURE

Barbara M. Chubbuck

Available from Amazon.com, Createspace.com, on Kindle and other retail outlets.

ISBN-13: 978-1508920458
ISBN-10: 1508920451
CreateSpace Independent Publishing Platform,
North Charleston, South Carolina

In loving memory of Joseph Michael

⌘

"If every time I thought of you, a star fell,
well, the sky would be empty." — **Unknown Author**

Acknowledgments

To my beloved son, Joseph Michael: Your unwavering strength and resilient faith throughout your battle with cancer will forever amaze me. You will never be forgotten Sunshine.

To my Heavenly father: Thank you for all the love and support shown to me throughout Joseph's illness and during my time of loss.

To my husband, Joe, my beautiful daughter, Alicia Marie, and my son-in-law, Brandon Alexander: Thank you for being such a strong family unit. Your love carried Joseph and me though the hardest of times.

To Deborah: Thank you for reading and editing my manuscript. Your support was appreciated more than words can express.

To Carol: Thank you for the countless hours spent reading and formatting my manuscript. You are a dear friend that has my heart-felt gratitude.

To those who support The Joseph Michael Chubbuck Foundation: Thank you. Joseph wanted to help other cancer patients and their families and your support makes this possible.

Contents

July 2013

He looked deep into my eyes and said, "I'm sorry I can't take your pain away, Mama." I wrapped my arms around him as the tears I had been holding back streamed down my cheeks. I said, "I wish I could trade places with you." He replied "I would never wish that on you or anybody else. I want you to live a long and full life...to have fun for at least another forty years." I said, "Forty years without you would be far too long, I would miss you too much. I can't imagine my life without you." He put his arms around me, gently kissed me on the forehead, and whispered, "You'll have to."

1
The Perfect Life

"Everything that looks too perfect is too perfect to be perfect."
— Dejan Stojanovic

Where do I begin? I close my eyes and wish it were a nightmare, a long terrible dream I will awaken from with profound relief. But, this will not happen, no matter how hard I pray for it. For this is not a dream, but the cold harsh reality of life – a strong slap in the face of how finite we are and how suddenly life can change.

In 2010, my daughter, Alicia Marie, was twenty-one years old and my son, Joseph Michael, was nineteen years old. Both were living on their own, working, and attending college full time. Alicia was majoring in Business Administration and Health Studies. Joseph was majoring in Physics.

In November of 2010, Joey enlisted in the Army National Guard with acceptance into Officer Candidate School. He left for boot camp the following May. He was fortunate enough to complete basic training just two days before Alicia's wedding. My husband, Joe, and I flew down to South Carolina to see him graduate on August 11th. We flew back with him in time to celebrate Alicia's 22nd birthday on August 12th and her wedding the proceeding day.

On Alicia's wedding day, Joey proudly served as a groomsmen. He looked handsome in his Army dress uniform. During the reception, Alicia had a brother-sister dance as a surprise for Joey. I can still remember the expression on Joey's face when the DJ called PVT First Class Joseph Chubbuck to the dance floor. Alicia beamed with pride as they danced to My Wish, by Rascal Flatts.

Prior to her wedding, Alicia had told me how much her brother meant to her. She wanted him to be happy in his life and to know he would find that someone special just like she had. Her eyes filled with tears as she told me how much she loved her childhood with him. A childhood filled with snow fort building, tree climbing, and numerous pretend adventures. I told her I missed those days as well. Here she was getting married and Joey was getting ready for Officer Candidate School (OCS). Time had passed by so quickly. My babies had grown up in the blink of an eye.

The Nightmare Begins

By late January of 2012, Joe had moved back home in preparation for his departure to OCS. At night he liked to sleep on the living room couch. In the mornings, I would find wet tee shirts on the floor drenched with sweat. Thinking the culprit was the fleece blanket he slept under, I ignored the sign and went about business as usual. By early February, I began to notice Joey's weight loss and declining appetite. When asked about them, he said he was in training for Officer Candidate School. As time passed his face became paler and his eyes became darker. Every time I asked him to see a doctor he refused. He didn't want to miss out on OCS.

On his twenty-first birthday, Sunday, March 11th, his two best friends came over to hang out with him. Twenty-one is the legal drinking age in New York State and Joey had been looking forward to celebrating his birthday with them. We all knew something was terribly wrong when Joey wasn't the slightest bit interested in going out. His friends asked me what was up. I told them I didn't know, but I was going to find out.

The next morning, I called our family physician and explained the situation. He said he wanted to see Joey immediately. Joey went to his office as I anxiously waited at home. Several hours passed before his return. He told me the doctor suspected something was wrong and had ordered blood work. As his blood was being drawn, he began to black out. This had never happened to him before, so the phlebotomist called the doctor. The doctor scripted an additional test for mononucleosis. Now, we had to wait for the results. With the exhaustion and fatigue he had been experiencing for the past few weeks, I suspected mononucleosis.

On March 14th, I came home from work to find Joey struggling to walk across the living room. He was hunched over and couldn't straighten up. I asked him what was wrong. He told me he was having pain on his lower right side. Suspecting appendicitis, I told him we needed to take him to the emergency room. On route to the ER, I called our physician. He told me he wanted Joey to have a CT scan because his blood results had came back abnormal. After hearing the news, Joey consented to the scan. I knew Alicia was worried about her brother, so I called her to let her know where we were heading.

At the ER, Joey drank iodine mixed in apple juice for the CT scan, which added to his intestinal discomfort. Despite the pain he was experiencing, Joey managed to walk to and from the bathroom down the hall. Initially, his upright posture caused the surgeon to doubt appendicitis. However, upon further evaluation, Joey's appendix proved to be inflamed and needed immediate removal. The surgeon told Joey he was impressed by his pain threshold. According to him, most people couldn't walk during a severe case of appendicitis.

As the staff was preparing to take Joey to surgery, the ER doctor came in with the scan results. She was visibly shaken. According to her, the radiologist wasn't certain what he was looking at. He told her he had never seen anything like it. Joey's abdomen appeared to be blanketed in some form of cancer. According to the scan, he had a softball size mass in the pelvis, fluid around the liver, possible cirrhosis, and several small masses diffused throughout the abdomen. We were stunned. I looked over at Joey. He was staring at the doctor with an expression of disbelief. The surgeon touched his shoulder saying, "I'll know more when I have a look inside."

As Joey was taken into surgery, we paced back and forth in the waiting room. In less than fifteen minutes, the surgeon came to see us. His facial expression told us all we needed to know. Joey's abdomen was full of cancer. The cancer had wrapped itself around the appendix resulting in appendicitis. The surgeon was able to remove the appendix and retrieve several sizable biopsies. We quizzed him – had he seen anything like this before, what type of cancer was it, was it treatable? He told us he had seen this type of cancer before, but not in someone Joey's age. He said, "I'm sorry, but his prognosis isn't good. The pathology report should tell us more once we get it back in seven to ten days."

As he walked away, we fell to pieces. Thank God no one was in the waiting room except Alicia and her husband, Brandon. We shared the devastating news with them. Overwhelmed with grief, I begged the Lord not to take my son. With unbelieving, tear-filled eyes Brandon held Alicia as she cried. Joe gazed out the window into the darkness, as he struggled to accept the news. My head was reeling with all sorts of thoughts and emotions. I asked myself if this was really happening. Then I thought, how am I going to tell Joey?

Sharing the News

Joey was in recovery for less than an hour when we were escorted in to see him. His father and I walked up to his bedside and stood to his left. Alicia stood to his right. Because Brandon was having a difficult time with his emotions, he stood several feet behind Alicia. Not the family photo anyone likes to envision.

Slowly, Joey opened his soft brown eyes and glanced around the room at each of us. Seeing Brandon standing behind Alicia he invited him to come closer saying, "You're part of the family now Bro, come on up here." Brandon managed to grin as he came forward beside Alicia. Joey looked at me and asked what the surgeon had found. I placed my hand over his and told him what the surgeon had said. He gazed down as he gently squeezed my hand. He told us he had suspected something major because of how he had been feeling. He asked what the next step would be. Joe told him the surgeon was sending the biopsies out for identification. This would take seven to ten days. After which, we should know more.

We remained in the recovery room for another hour before Joey was transferred to a hospital room. After settling in, he asked us to go home and get some rest. On the drive home, Joe and I cried. Our perfect life had been shattered the moment we heard our son had cancer.

2

The Days & Weeks That Followed

"Today we fight. Tomorrow we fight. The day after, we fight.
And if this disease plans on whipping us, it better bring a lunch,
'cause it's gonna have a long day doing it.
— Jim Beaver, Life's That Way A Memoir

The morning after Joey's emergency surgery, we shared the news with our families. Everyone was in shock. How could Joey have cancer? The surgeon told us the biopsy samples had been sent to Sloan Kettering, Roswell Park, and the Mayo Clinic. The cancer was severe enough that he recommended the placement of a chemotherapy port.

On March 19th, Joey was taken into surgery and a port was placed in his upper right chest. A few days after the port surgery, a local oncologist came to see Joey. He introduced himself and told Joey he felt he had a very bad form of cancer, possibly carcinoid. This type of cancer, most likely, would end his life within a year despite treatment. I asked him the basis of his prognosis. He told me he didn't have the pathology report yet, but he had spoken with the surgeon. I wondered why he would tell a twenty-one year old patient such devastating news without any pathologic evidence. Before departing, he offered Joey his services and left his business card.

Joey told us he didn't like the oncologist's demeanor. He wanted to wait for the pathology reports and get a second opinion. When an individual is facing a situation like his, you want a doctor with some optimism. You don't want a doctor telling you there is no hope without supportive evidence. I called our physician and told him we needed to find Joey the best possible care. To do this, we needed a committed, positive doctor. He told me he would discuss the matter with his wife, Beth, a general surgeon, who had a lot of connections in the area. The next morning his wife called. She told me she wanted to help Joey. Beth is a very optimistic, yet realistic person. Exactly the combination Joey was looking for.

Waiting is the hardest part when you know something is growing inside your son's body silently killing him with each tick of the clock. I remained humbled by Joey's composure. We would have imploded without his strength. Every night, I prayed the Lord would guide us to the right treatment in time to save his life.

Prior to Joey's diagnosis, I had been attending graduate classes for my administrative certificate in education. I had two classes left in the semester. I arrived early for class so I could talk privately with the professor. I explained the situation to her. She proceeded to tell me her brother-in-law had a similar occurrence a few years before. She told me he underwent a new type of surgery, followed by chemotherapy, at Sloan Kettering. Currently, he was in remission. A twinge of hope rushed through me. Could Joey have this treatment and achieve remission? She told me she would ask her sister for the name and number of the doctor. That evening, she called with the specialist's information. I was so excited – I could barely wait to call Beth in the morning.

At 9AM, I called Beth's office. She sounded as excited as I was over the news. She had her associate call the specialist and explain Joey's situation to him. The specialist asked for a copy of Joey's medical records and CT scan. Later that afternoon, he called back. He said, "If this were my son, I would get him to Dr. David Bartlett at UPMC in Pittsburgh, PA, as soon as possible." Beth called me with the news. She told me she would make a timely appointment with Dr. Bartlett.

Meanwhile, the specialist recommended that Joey have an endoscopy to make sure the cancer wasn't inside his stomach. Joey was scheduled for an endoscopy the next morning. Thankfully, no evidence of cancer was found in his stomach or esophagus.

Consultation in Pittsburgh

Joey was discharged on March 21, 2012. By March 24th, he was in rough shape. He was taking Oxycodone for pain and his spleen was inflamed. His lips were pale and his skin was jaundiced. He told me he felt lousy and he was scared. He knew something had to be done and soon. I hugged him and said, "We're all scared, Joey. Try to hang in there." Again, I prayed for guidance and help.

We drove to the Hillman Cancer Center in Pittsburgh, PA, the last week of March for Joey's consultation with Dr. Bartlett. We arrived the night before and stayed at the Shadyside Marriott, located just minutes from the cancer center. Needless-to-say, none of us slept well. We were dressed and ready to go early the next morning. We took the hotel shuttle to the cancer center because Joey was too weak to walk any distance.

As we entered the center, I took in the sights and sounds. The hair salon with wigs displayed in the window, the gift shop with cancer themed tee shirts, and patients talking about their various stages of treatment. The whole experience was surreal – I just couldn't believe we were there with our son.

We waited fifteen minutes before we were brought into an exam room. Dr. Bartlett's physician assistant introduced herself and said, "We received all of Joseph's records." She reviewed Joey's medical history and told us Dr. Bartlett would be in shortly. A few minutes later, Dr. Bartlett entered the room and shook our hands. He had already reviewed Joey's medical history, pathology reports, and CT scan. He told us Joey was a strong candidate for a relatively new surgical procedure known as HIPEC (Hyperthermic Intraperitoneal Chemotherapy). He had been using this state-of-the art surgery for some time at UPMC. The surgical procedure involves debulking of the tumor followed by heated chemotherapy infused into and circulated throughout the intraperitoneal (abdominal) cavity for ninety minutes. The chemotherapy drug Cisplatin would be used on Joey. This particular drug is hard on the kidneys; therefore, Joey would be given large amounts of IV fluids after the surgery to prevent kidney failure.

To our amazement, he stated Joey's preliminary pathology report indicated he had mesothelioma. We were stunned. How could Joey get a cancer caused by asbestos when he was never near any, let alone at such a young age? Dr. Bartlett told us, though it was an uncommon event, he had operated on young adults with mesothelioma before. Since Joey was a member of the Army National Guard, he asked if he had ever been deployed out of the country where he could have been exposed to other chemicals or gases. Joey told him he hadn't been deployed. The only gas he had been exposed to was the gas used in the boot camp gas chambers. Dr. Bartlett said exposure to that particular gas wouldn't have caused his current condition.

Dr. Bartlett went on to explain all the possible postsurgical complications. He stressed the need to act quickly given Joey's current condition, so Joey's surgery was scheduled for Monday, April

9th. It would be at Passavant Hospital in northern Pittsburgh. We decided to return home and come back to Pittsburgh the weekend of the surgery.

Back home, I called Passavant Hospital and was given housing options for a long-term stay. We opted to rent a first floor apartment at The Woodhawk Club starting the weekend of the surgery. The complex was located less than ten miles from the hospital.

The HIPEC Surgery

Thank God the surgery was scheduled as soon as it was. Joey's condition was rapidly deteriorating. Beth was worried his spleen would rupture before he got to Pittsburgh for surgery. She kept a close eye on him up until our departure on April 6th.

We arrived at the Woodhawk Club Apartment early that evening. The apartment was fully furnished with two bedrooms and two bathrooms. Alicia and Brandon stayed with Joey while Joe and I purchased food and toiletries at a nearby grocery store. We settled in with the expectation of being in Pittsburgh for two to three weeks.

The night before the surgery, none of us were able to sleep. Joey had to do a bowel prep to clean out his intestines. This, in combination with the abdominal pain he was already experiencing, made his night miserable. We couldn't do or say anything to comfort him. As I lay in bed, I found myself praying for the surgery to go well and hoping Joey would be strong enough to beat this cancer.

By 4AM, we were awake and preparing to go to the hospital. My stomach was in knots and my irritable bowel was kicking in. I had been prescribed Valium, so I took half a pill. The early morning ride to the hospital was filled with apprehension and stress. Not one of us spoke. Upon arrival, Joey checked in at the admissions desk and the receptionist told him to report to the surgical floor using the adjacent elevators.

Shortly after our arrival on the surgery floor, around 5:20AM, a nurse called Joey's name. We were escorted down a long hallway into a small exam room. The nurse told us we could take a few minutes to wish Joey luck before he was taken into pre-op. Alicia, Joe, and I told Joey we loved him and gave him a hug and kiss. Brandon wished him luck and gave him a hug. Joey gave each of us a slight smile as he told us he loved us. He looked tired and worn, and his battle had just begun. I walked down the hall to the waiting room with a lump in my throat and tears in my eyes. I couldn't begin to imagine how Joey was feeling.

In the surgical waiting room, we were given a number. The number would be used to track Joey in the surgery process. We found his number on one of the monitors and it indicated he was in pre-op. I had read about the HIPEC surgery on the UPMC website. I knew that pre-op would be the time when Joey would change out of his street clothes and into a hospital gown, have an IV started for fluids, be given a mild sedative, nerve blocks would be explained by the pain team, he would meet with the anesthesiologist, and his vitals would be assessed. After that, he would be taken into the surgery suite where he would be fully sedated, intubated, and placed on several monitors.

After which, he would be surgically prepped and the surgery would begin. The first part of the surgery would be exploratory laparoscopy to assess whether the debulking and chemo-perfusion surgery should commence.

At 7:30AM, Joey's number indicated he was in surgery. As we waited, I prayed the rosary and visited the chapel several times. I asked the Lord to save my son and to guide the surgeon's hands. About two hours after the surgery began, a volunteer in the surgical waiting room called me to the front desk. She handed me a phone and said, "You have a phone call from the operating room." I placed the phone to my ear saying, "This is Barb Chubbuck." I heard a woman's voice say, "The doctor is proceeding with the surgery Mrs. Chubbuck." I thanked her and hung up. I walked back to my seat and shared the news with my family.

Joey's surgery lasted twelve hours...the longest twelve hours of our lives. I could feel the tension in the air. We had been the first family to arrive in the surgery waiting room that morning. Now, we were the last to remain. The janitor had cleaned the room in preparation for the next day, the lighting had been dimmed, and the staff at the front desk had left. I remember thinking, "What's happening in that surgery suit and will Joey's body be able to handle it once it's over?"

Finally, a surgical nurse appeared from behind the double doors. She asked if we were the Chubbuck family. I said, "Yes." She told us Joey was out of surgery and the doctor would be out to see us shortly. After what seemed a lifetime, Dr. Bartlett walked through the double doors. I recall thinking the moment seemed like a scene from a movie – the doctor coming to share the greatly anticipated news with the distraught family. But this was not a movie.

Dr. Bartlett looked tired, but focused. He looked at each of us with compassion as he explained what had been done in the surgical process. He said he was able to remove all visible tumor, but there was a great deal of it. Much more than the scan had revealed. To debulk the tumor, he had to remove all the peritoneal lining in Joey's abdominal cavity from the diaphragm downward because the tumor was growing along the lining. He said these types of tumors grow like sheets across the tissues in the body. The tumor seeds and spreads itself along the lining of all the organs and tissues it contacts. Because of this, he had to remove all of Joey's spleen, a lobe of his liver, three centimeters of his stomach, a portion of small intestine, a portion of large intestine, and some of his rectum. He also removed several small masses throughout Joey's abdomen along with a softball size pelvic mass. In order for his rectal area to heal properly, he had to give Joey a temporary ileostomy (an opening made in the abdomen where the small bowel exits through the outside of the body into a bag).

After hearing all of this, we couldn't believe how much tumor had grown in Joey's abdomen without him ever experiencing any symptoms. How could this be possible? How long had this monster been lurking inside of him?

Dr. Bartlett told us Joey handled the procedure well, but he would be in ICU for a few days. Currently, he was on a ventilator because the surgery was long and his body was tired. He told us Joey would need chemotherapy because the cancer had infiltrated a few abdominal lymph nodes. He had sent the nodes out for analysis. Joe said, "The surgery seemed to be as successful as possible Doc, given all visible cancer was removed. That in itself is a miracle." We all agreed.

Dr. Bartlett told us a nurse would call us once Joey was settled in the ICU. We thanked him and tried to convey our gratitude. As he walked away, I asked God to bless him for all he had done for our son. Now, came the hard part, seeing Joey in ICU.

Intensive Care

Nothing prepares a parent for seeing their child in ICU, let alone on a ventilator. When we entered the ICU room, Joey's nurse explained all the tubes and monitors attached to him - pulse, respiration, temperature, oxygen, and heart rate. She told us he would be highly sedated for pain, but would be more conscious in the morning. If he remained stable, the doctors would wean him off the ventilator in the morning.

Looking down at my son, I was overcome by how frail he looked. I gently lifted one of his hands and placed it in mine. Alicia stood across from me, gently rubbing the top of Joey's other hand with her fingers. We both struggled to maintain our composure. Joe took one look at Joey and walked past him to the window. He stood there a few moments before returning to Joey's side. Brandon stood at the foot of the bed. The reality of what Joey was up against was apparent to us. How could Joey be in this position? Just a few months ago, he was at the top of his game, on the verge of making his mark in this world. Now, he was fighting for his life.

As I looked down at Joey, I flashed back to him as a little boy playing in the backyard. Then, I envisioned him strong and healthy in his dress uniform walking me down the aisle just eight months before. How much I wanted to trade places with him, to comfort him, to take this nightmare away. In my head, one phrase kept repeating itself, "Why Lord, why?"

The nurse said some patients under sedation remember what their loved ones said to them, so we wanted Joey to know we were there. We told him the surgery went well, we loved him, and he was doing great. We told him how proud we were of him. Joey never opened his eyes that night. All we heard was the steady drone of the ventilator.

Around 1AM, the nurse told us we needed to get some rest. She assured me she would call my cell phone should anything change. Reluctantly, we left the ICU and went to the apartment for a few hours sleep.

Behind closed doors, in our bedroom, I cried. I dropped to my knees...asking God why my son had to have this happen to him. Why he had to suffer like this. I remember thinking, "This is what heartache feels like." I thought about the Blessed Mother and how she must have felt seeing Jesus suffer. I was sure she understood my pain.

It was late, but I phoned my mom. She told me she had been waiting for my call. I told her about the surgery and asked her to pray for Joey. She told me he was a strong young man and God would be with him. She told me not to lose faith because I needed to be strong for him.

After hanging up the phone, I thanked God for allowing the surgery to go as well as it had, for guiding us to an amazing surgeon. Then, Joe and I prayed the first of many nightly rosaries – asking Our Lady for her mercy and her help.

Complications after Surgery

The next morning, I awoke with abdominal pain. I told Joe I was having sympathy pains. He never questioned me. He got dressed and drove me to the hospital. When we arrived at the ICU, Joey was awake and in considerable pain. I kissed his forehead and tried to comfort him by holding his hand. His wrists were loosely strapped down to his sides, he had cloth mitts over his hands, and slight tears were coming down his cheeks. His nurse said he was in a great deal of discomfort because he had declined the nerve blocks prior to surgery. He had been reaching for the ventilator tube, so she had to restrain him.

Joey couldn't talk. Anxiety flashed in his eyes as he gagged on the tube. I said, "Try not to fight it Joey. Try to relax and let the machine breath for you sweetie." His nurse did a great job talking to him, comforting him, and getting his pain down to a tolerable level.

As Joey was being weaned off the ventilator, he started to gag from the buildup of mucous in his throat. He motioned his head toward a nearby suction tool. The nurse undid one of the restraints, took his mitt off, and handed him the suction tool. Joey stuck the tool down his throat to suck up the mucous. She said, "You're a strong patient. Not many people can do that to themselves."

By mid-morning, Joey had successfully weaned himself off the ventilator. He said, "I'm so glad to be off that damn thing. It's hard to relax and let the machine breath for you." I can only imagine. To this day, I am haunted by the sound of a ventilator.

As the day progressed Joey's pain began to intensify. His heart rate and blood pressure steadily increased, despite high dosages of pain medication. The doctors changed his pain medication and added a blood pressure medication. This adjustment worked well as long as the medications were given around the clock.

On April 11th, we arrived at the ICU to find Joey weak and struggling to breathe. The pulmonary doctors told us he was having sudden tachycardia, rapid heart rate, due to his chest cavity filling with excess fluid. After the HIPEC surgery he was given large amounts of IV fluid to prevent kidney failure. Some of the excess fluid was leaving his bloodstream and filling the empty body spaces around his lungs. Joey had to have this fluid drained or his lungs would collapse. To make matters worse, the excess fluid had caused a buildup of carbon dioxide in Joey's blood making him delirious.

He was refusing to sign the consent form for the emergency chest tube placements. He was asking to see his lawyer and speaking to the pulmonary doctor as if he were one of his military commanders.

I tried to reason with him, but he was too confused. I was his power of attorney, so I asked if I could sign the form. The doctor said

I couldn't because Joey was considered competent. He offered to page a psychologist to have Joey evaluated. But this would take time. We knew Joey needed the procedure as soon as possible. We were beside ourselves. What could we do?

I grabbed my cell phone and called Beth. I knew Joey trusted her. Thankfully, she picked up on the first ring. I explained the situation to her. She told me to put my phone to Joey's ear. I heard her speaking to Joey, but I couldn't make out her words. Joey mumbled back. Then, he told the nurse he would sign the consent. He took the pen and scribbled something to their satisfaction. Thank God for Beth.

After they obtained Joey's signature, the pulmonologist had Joey sit up. He opened the back of his gown and asked us to leave the room. Later, Joey told us the doctor made two small incisions in his back and inserted small tubes into his chest. He was given a local anesthetic, but the procedure was still painful. I told him we felt helpless standing on the sidelines. He said not to feel bad because he was too sick to give a damn. He had no recollection of the delirium, but he did remember thinking he was going to die.

As the tubes were inserted, a liter of fluid was drained from one side of his chest and half a liter from the other. An x-ray was taken to verify the tube placements and another problem was discovered. Joey had a pulmonary embolism, a blood clot in one of his lungs.

The discovery of the clot led to the immediate placement of an IVC filter. This filter is inserted through a vein in the groin to prevent clots from traveling to the lungs or heart. The placement of the IVC filter took place in a sterile surgical suite with the aid of a radiologist. Joey told us the procedure involved covering his entire body in a plastic sheet to ensure a sterile environment. The doctor gave him IV pain medication and a local anesthetic injection in the groin before inserting a small device through a blood vessel in his groin. The procedure took less than an hour.

Needless to say, all of Joey's post-surgical complications were sending us into a panic. We began to wonder if he had the strength to endure all that was happening to him.

Factor V Leiden

A niece on my husband's side has Factor Five Leiden. This is a genetic mutation resulting in a higher risk of clotting problems.

Since Joey experienced the unexpected pulmonary embolism, we asked the doctors to test him for the factor. The doctors agreed.

Joey tested positive for carrying one panel of the mutation. This meant Joey needed to stay on blood thinners throughout his cancer treatment. Thankfully, from that point on, his condition began to improve.

Up and Walking

On April 13th his nurse, Kim, said it was time for Joey to walk. She brought in a weird box-like contraption on wheels with an attached seat. Joey would stand up inside the box, grip the walking rails, and walk around the unit. If he got tired he could sit for a moment on the attached seat.

To our amazement, Joey was able to do a complete lap around the ICU without having to sit. Kim managed to make him laugh a few times, which hurt his incision more than the walking. Brandon joined in the fun by using his cell phone to time Joey's laps around the unit. It felt good to see Joey up on his feet and walking again.

Kim was Joey's nurse for several days and she was great. She addressed Joey's physical and mental wellbeing. She would get Joey to talk about his illness. He told her he was not certain of his future but he was going to fight as hard as he could. He communicated one wish to Kim – he didn't want people to treat him differently. Kim told him that people were bound to treat him differently because they felt bad for him. He would have to understand that. She told him he had to let people know how he felt. In other words, he had to address the elephant in the room – his cancer. We thanked her for all she had done.

With Joey steadily improving, Alicia and Brandon decided to return home. After ten days in ICU, Joey was transferred to a hospital room on 6 PAV. Kim told him to keep walking and she would be up to visit when she wasn't on duty.

6 PAV

A few days after Joey's arrival on 6 PAV, he started to spike a fever. The attending physician quickly evaluated him. He ordered blood work, blood cultures, a chest x-ray, and an abdominal scan. The tests quickly identified the problem - two pockets of bacterial fluid in his abdomen. To stop the infection, Joey had to undergo surgery to place drain tubes in each side of his abdomen.

After the surgery, Joey showed us the drains. Each drain was a clear tube about the size of a cocktail straw stitched in place about three inches from his belly button on either side. Each tube ended in a clear plastic grenade. The grenades could be squeezed to pull the fluid out from the pockets in his body. Nurses would measure the amount of fluid in the drains and empty them throughout the day. In addition to the drains, Joey was given several IV antibiotics as the fluid contained several types of bacteria. Some of the antibiotics didn't agree with Joey's stomach, so he was given various nausea medications.

When Joey had his HIPEC surgery, a mid-line incision was made from the bottom of his breastbone to the top of his pelvis area, approximately ten inches in length. This area was stitched underneath and stapled on top. Alicia counted over fifty staples. As this mid-line incision healed, it was under the supervision of wound care nurses. A wound care nurse would come in twice a week to change the bandages, observe the wound, and make treatment recommendations.

A few weeks after Joey's surgery, a wound nurse noted a fluid build-up in a few areas of the incision. She recommended the removal of the staples in those areas and the placement of a wound vac. The next day Joey had the staples removed and a wound vac placed on the wound.

The wound vac is an interesting device made up of a large sterile black sponge cut to size and inserted down into the open wound. The sponge is attached to a powered vacuum canister by a sealed clear tube. The suction pulls the sponge down into the wound and drains the fluids from the wound into the canister. This device has been proven to speed up healing in deep wounds. Joey said the vac felt like the end of a vacuum hose stuck to your skin. He had to wear the device 24/7. Thankfully, it was portable so we were able to leave the room for short walks.

Joey and I stayed on 6 PAV for two and a half weeks. One nurse, Ranjit, was kind enough to give me a cot with bedding. This enabled me to sleep in Joey's room every night. Once a day, I would drive to the apartment to take a shower and exchange garments. I have to admit it was a long two and a half weeks, but I wouldn't change a thing. I promised Joey when he was diagnosed that I would never leave his side. I was going to keep that promise.

Pathology Problems

A few weeks after Joey's HIPEC surgery, the pathology results arrived. Dr. Bartlett told us the pathologists no longer felt Joey had mesothelioma because the morphology of the tumor didn't quite match. The problem was the pathologists didn't know for certain what type of cancer Joey had. The pathology reports from the other cancer institutes shared the same results. Our question was simple, "How can an oncologist treat Joey's cancer if the pathologists aren't certain what type it is?" He told us the UPMC pathologists were continuing to study stained slides for evidence of tumor type. Meanwhile, Joey should use this time to heal. Hopefully an answer would present itself in the near future.

Treatment Away From Home

Having Joey's treatment in Pittsburgh was hardest on Alicia and Joe because they had to travel back and forth from home. Alicia had a new job and Joe was needed at the family business. I, on the other hand, was fortunate. My employer, Waterville Central School, had approved my request for a leave of absence.

The whole situation was a challenge, but we managed to develop a routine. Joe would work all week and drive to Pittsburgh every Friday night. He would stay with Joey and me until late Sunday morning. Alicia would come down on weekends as often as she could. If she came alone, she would sleep on the cot in Joey's room at night. Her father and I would stay at the apartment. We all agreed time together was the one positive aspect of this entire nightmare. We had always been a close family. Now, we were getting even closer.

Precious Time

I slept on a cot in Joey's room at night because this enabled me to comfort him when he wasn't feeling well and coordinate his care with the nurses/doctors. I was there for around the clock moral support. I thought of myself as his primary caregiver and patient advocate. Joey was relieved because he didn't have to worry about me being alone in the apartment at night.

Joey and I created a lifetime of memories in the weeks we spent together. We talked about life, faith, his childhood, the future, and his cancer. Some days I couldn't fathom what the future held for him. I seemed to have a constant ache in my heart. I said a Novena to the Blessed Mother twice a day. Every night, before bed, I would say the rosary. I was scared. I knew the road ahead was going to be long and difficult. Joey had endured so much already and he still had to endure aggressive chemotherapy.

Some nights Joey felt awful. He would say, "I don't know if I am going to make it Mom." On those nights I would hold him close, lightly kiss his forehead, and tell him to keep the faith. I would say,

"I'm so proud of you, Sunshine." I knew my words brought him comfort, but I wished they could have given him more. This time with Joey was precious to me.

Despicable Ileostomy

Joey hated the ileostomy with a passion. He would eat and the food would pour right out of him in to the attached bag. Sometimes he would swallow a pill only to find it in his bag a few minutes later. He struggled to stay hydrated. To slow the motility of food down, he took three Lomotil and ten Imodium AD tablets per day. Still, the nutrients passed through him.

Both of us were trained to change his ileostomy bag and properly care for the site. Initially, I changed the ileostomy wafer and cleaned the site as instructed. Gradually, Joey took over the task.

Despite his effort to deal with the ileostomy, the bag had a profound negative psychological impact on him. He would sit and stare at it. On rare occasions, he would reiterate his hatred of having to change the bag and how the bag made him feel. Usually his intolerance manifested itself through a simple outburst followed by an immediate apology. Everyone knew it was frustration talking because so much had happened to him so fast.

Trying to Cope

Most of the time, I didn't even know what to say to Joey to help him feel better. I couldn't say the usual responses like, "Don't worry it will all work out" or "Things will get better." All I could do was try to support him the best way I knew how. Sometimes this involved saying nothing at all. I would hold him when he would let me and I would keep my distance when asked to. I had to find a balance between treating him like my child and the young man he was.

Every day I would remind him how well he was handling the situation. Several times I called him *my hero*. One night when we were having one of our sentimental talks, I told him to ask God for help. He told me he did pray to God, but his prayers weren't for God to cure him. Instead, he asked that God's will be done. He told me he felt God had a plan for each of us. I told him I hated to see him suffer like this. He said, "Jesus suffered more than I have." This comment took me by surprise. I had always been a person of faith, but Joey never seemed to put much value in his faith. He graduated from Catholic school, but rarely attended mass after graduation. Often he would say, "You pray in your way Mom and I'll pray in mine." At that moment I thought, "Joey knows more about faith than I do. He has enough to turn his life over to God's will come what may."

Besides faith, Joe and I discussed life experiences, our future goals, and his cancer. We laughed together, prayed together, and cried together. We had always been close, but were becoming even closer. I was getting to know the young man in front of me. How quickly he had grown up.

Joey told me how badly he wanted to be married, to have a family of his own. Now, he didn't know if that would ever happen. My heart broke for him when he spoke like this. I knew he would be a great father and husband. I could only hope he would be given the chance. Amazingly, on all those nights we spent in conversation, I never heard resentment in his voice – only sadness and regret.

Discharged at Last

On May 7th Joey was discharged from Passavant Hospital. At this time, he weighed one hundred and eleven pounds. He had lost over thirty-five pounds since his diagnosis in March. His post-hospital checkup was scheduled for May 10th, so we remained in Pittsburgh at our Woodhawk Club apartment.

The check up went well. Joey's incision was healing with the help of the wound vac and his pain was well managed. Dr. Bartlett told us the pathologists were still having trouble identifying the type of cancer. He asked if we could remain in Pittsburgh for another week and meet with him again on May 17th.

In the days that followed, Joey had difficulty with the ileostomy and one of his drains. He told me he was noticing blood in the right drain tube. A nurse at Dr. Bartlett's office told me to take Joey to the Passavant ER so the drain could be assessed.

At the ER, Joey was evaluated. The doctor placed Joey on IV fluids for dehydration and ordered an abdominal CT scan. The scan revealed the blood was coming from the abdominal abscess area. In the absence of infection, the body was draining blood. The doctor gently cut the stitches and removed the drain tube from Joey's right side. He left the second drain tube in place because there was still a pocket of infection in that area. He told Joey this would be a good time for him to have his IVC filter removed. Joey agreed. So, Joey was admitted.

On May 14th the IVC filter was removed without incident. Joey remained in the hospital twenty-four hours post-procedure.

The Follow-up

On May 17th, I drove Joey to the Hillman Cancer Center for his scheduled appointment. Dr. Bartlett introduced us to a team of oncologists. One oncologist told us the pathologists at UPMC believed Joey's cancer was a type of sarcoma known as small blue round cell tumor. He told Joey his wounds would have to heal before any chemo could be given. With that said, Dr. Bartlett told Joey to return home to heal and he would be contacted with possible treatment options in the near future.

Joey and I headed home on May 18th. We were excited to see our house, our dogs, our family, and our friends. Most of all, we looked forward to sleeping in our own beds. Joey told me he would take this time to prepare himself for aggressive chemotherapy. I would use the time to lean on family and friends. Take my advice, to get through something like this you have to take one day at a time...to look at the whole picture would be too overwhelming.

Homecoming Scare

The afternoon of May 18th, I drove Joey from Pittsburgh to Buffalo. I decided to spend the night in Buffalo because I was exhausted from loading the car and taking care of Joey. I had been cleaning Joey's abdominal wound and ileostomy site, administering his IV antibiotics, injecting his blood thinner, hooking up his IV fluids, and managing his many medications throughout the day. I was also keeping track of his ileostomy and urine output for the home care nurse.

At the hospital, the nurses did all of these various tasks around the clock so I was able to get some rest. Now, all these tasks were left to me. I was tired and stressed out. On occasion Joey would get grumpy with me. I tried my best to remain patient with him, but there were moments when I thought I might lose the edge altogether.

Upon check in, I discovered there were no rooms available on the first floor of the hotel. So, I helped Joey walk up the stairs to our room on the second floor. I made sure he was comfortable before returning to the car. I unloaded the suitcases, along with Joey's overnight medical supplies, and carried them up to our room. We ate a light meal, watched some television, and decided to go to bed early.

A few hours later, I woke up with my heart pounding in my chest. I felt nauseous, light headed, and dizzy. I reached over and took Joey's blood pressure kit off the nightstand. My blood pressure was sky high. I started to experience shortness of breath. Was I having a heart attack?

I glanced at the clock – 2AM. Joey was sound asleep in the adjacent bed. I decided not to wake him because he was too weak to help.

I grabbed my phone and called Beth. I apologized for waking her and explained the situation. She asked me if I had Valium. I did. She told me to take one pill and lay down on the floor. After a few minutes, she told me to take my blood pressure. The reading had dropped. She said I was probably having an anxiety attack from all the stress I had been under. She told me to get some rest and to dial 911 should the symptoms return. She would order an echocardiogram when I got home. I thanked her before ending the call. Though I was scared, I could tell the Valium was taking effect. Gradually, the nausea subsided. I climbed back into bed and fell asleep.

The next morning, I had some nausea as I loaded the car and helped Joey get settled in the front seat. I didn't tell him anything about the night's events because he was dealing with enough. I just wanted to get home. I was scared of having another episode on the road. Three hours later we pulled into our driveway as I breathed a sigh of relief.

Home at Last

How great it felt to be home, especially with Joey looking better than he had in months. Yes, the cancer was still in our lives, but it felt good to see Joey watching his favorite movies as he lay on the living room couch. Every so often, I would get a text message from his nurses. Kim or Ranjit would ask how 'their Joey' was doing.

Kim would jokingly ask if he was walking. Ranjit would tell me she was praying for Joey at her temple. She told me how he touched her heart when she walked into his hospital room and he was so polite to her, despite the condition he was in. His humility made her cry. Both nurses held a special place in Joey's heart and ours.

Joey and I enjoyed six weeks at home, but those weeks were far from normal. A home care nurse came to change his port needle, check his wound, and draw his blood weekly. I would keep track of his urine and ileostomy output, give him his oral medications, and administer his IV antibiotics. Due to the summer heat, he struggled with dehydration and was hospitalized twice.

Roswell Park Cancer Institute

Mid-June, Joey received a phone call from the Pitt oncologist. He told Joey he had set up an appointment for him with an oncologist at Roswell Park on June 20th. He had selected Roswell due to its proximity to our home. He told Joey he was welcome to return to Pittsburgh if he didn't like the oncologist at Roswell.

He told Joey the UPMC pathologist felt his cancer was a rare type of sarcoma known as DSRCT, Desmoplastic Small Round Cell Tumor. This cancer usually occurs in children and young adults, and is more common in males. The pathologists based their conclusion on a chromosomal mutation commonly seen within DSRCT known as EWSR1. Joey's tumor had the EWSR1 mutation within it. This form of cancer has no known cure so his goal was to start Joey on chemo to prolong his life. Of course, this news was upsetting. Who wants to hear they are facing a rare, aggressive, and incurable cancer?

Thankfully, Joey had a close friend who had a rare blood disorder, aplastic anemia, who was recently cured. She was told her disease was incurable and would limit her life expectancy. Just over a year ago, she had undergone a new stem cell treatment at the National Institute of Health. Now, she was one of three individuals in the nation to be cured. Certainly this helped Joey realize the impossible could be possible. Why couldn't he be the first person cured with DSRCT? He knew he needed to find the best available treatment, even if it meant participation in clinical trials. Joe and I began to read current research on DSRCT and all the possible treatment options. Our goal was to stay positive. Hope, Faith, and Love became our family motto.

On June 20th, Joey, Joe, and I traveled to Roswell Park for our scheduled meeting with the sarcoma specialist. He reviewed Joey's case and told us how he would treat the cancer, if it were DSRCT. He told us the pathologist at Roswell didn't agree with the pathologist's report from UPMC. Again, we found ourselves asking, "How do you treat what can't be identified?" He told us he needed a current assessment of the cancer growth in Joey's abdomen so he sent Joey to radiology for a CT scan.

Prior to the scan, Joey was asked to drink two bottles of flavored barium. He barely got half of the barium down due to the nausea it created. He told me he was concerned about the barium blocking his ileostomy. After his scan was completed, we returned to the oncologist's office to review the results.

The scan showed some recurrent tumor growth within the abdomen and pelvis, along with a possible reactive lymph node in the chest. He told Joey he was going to consult a doctor at Sloan Kettering and he may be sending him there for treatment. All three of us got the impression that he didn't feel comfortable treating Joey.

This made us nervous. I began to wonder if there was time to take Joey to another consultation now that the cancer was growing. How fast would the disease spread while he was waiting to see the oncologist at Sloan? I had tons of questions, but no answers. I just knew the clock was ticking and time was of the essence.

That evening, Joey's worse fear came true. He had very little output in his ileostomy bag and he began to experience considerable nausea. He believed the barium had hardened into a plug blocking his ileostomy. I called Beth. She told me to bring Joey to the hospital for an x-ray. A small blockage at the ileostomy site was confirmed. Joey was admitted to the hospital and put on nausea medication, IV fluids, and complete bowel rest.

This was the final straw for Joey. He told me he couldn't take living with the ileostomy any longer. He wanted the reversal surgery as soon as possible. I expressed our concern about him having the reversal. I told him another surgery would delay his chemo and give the cancer more time to advance in his body. He told me he understood the risk but he couldn't live like this any longer. He wanted some quality of life back even if it meant shortening his life in the end. He said, "It is my life Mom and my choice to make." He asked me to set up a consultation with Dr. Bartlett.

At twenty-one, Joey signed his own medical forms. As a parent, it is hard to give up control especially if you believe your child is making a compulsive decision. Nonetheless, I respected his wishes and a consultation was scheduled for July 5th. Joey asked his father and me to remain in the waiting room when he went in to discuss the reversal with Dr. Bartlett.

We drove to Pittsburgh on July 4th and spent the night at the Holiday Inn. The next morning, Joe and I remained seated in the waiting room when Joey's name was called. About thirty minutes later, Joey came out and told us the reversal surgery was being scheduled for July 11th. The surgical staff would be contacting me with the time, location, and other key information. As we left the office, I prayed Joey had made the right decision.

The Reversal

Luckily we were able to secure the same Woodhawk Club apartment, so Joey and I remained in Pittsburgh. Joe returned home.

The day before the surgery, Joey wasn't acting right. He was very quiet and slept on the couch. Mid-afternoon, he asked me if I wanted to see the new Spider Man movie. His request took me by surprise. The movie theater was nearby and we drove pass Passavant Hospital on the way. We arrived at the theater and purchased our tickets. About ten minutes into the movie, Joey said he had to use the restroom. I hated to let him go alone because he had experienced episodes of fainting from sudden drops in his blood pressure. But, I knew he would get mad if I followed him. So, I waited anxiously in my seat.

Less than ten minutes passed when I felt a tap on my shoulder. Joey said, "We have to go, Mom, I'm having chest pain." I asked him how long he had been having pain and how bad it felt. He told me he was having pain all morning, but it was getting worse. This upset and frustrated me. Joey had a pattern of keeping symptoms to himself until they were out of control. He was his own worst enemy. I shook my head, got up, and walked with him to the car.

I put the emergency flashers on and headed straight to the ER at Passavant. Upon arrival, I told the receptionist Joey's medical history and current symptoms. A nurse got a wheelchair and took Joey in to an exam room as I handled the paperwork. Joey explained his situation to the ER doctor as he was being hooked up to IV fluids. The doctor put Joey on pain medication and ordered an immediate EKG, chest x-ray, and CT scan. As Joey was undergoing the tests, I called home to share the news with Joe and Alicia. Both of them were planning on driving to Pittsburgh after work. Now, they would leave immediately.

When the ER doctor returned, he told Joey all his tests were clear. However, he was going to admit him for observation. When I knew Joey was no longer in danger of a heart attack or pulmonary embolism, I called Joe and Alicia to tell them the good news.

That evening, Dr. Ahrendt stopped in to discuss the reversal surgery. He told Joey he looked stable enough to have the scheduled procedure. So, the next morning, Joey went into surgery.

As Joey's surgery was commencing, the oncologist from Roswell Park called. He told me the pathologists there didn't suspect DSRCT but possibly another rare cancer. He didn't recommend getting a reversal prior to starting chemo. He felt the cancer should be addressed first in order to give Joey the best possible chance at long-term survival. My stomach flipped. I told him about the blocked ileostomy after Joey's visit and how he had decided to get the ileostomy reversed. I told him what Joey had said to us. He told me he understood where he was coming from. I said, "We are at Passavant Hospital now and Joey is in his reversal surgery." He said, "Please let me know the results of the surgery and where Joey wants to have his chemo done." I thanked him for calling and told him I would let him know. I ended the call thinking, "Did Joey's decision just cause him his life?"

Joey's reversal took three hours, but he was strong enough to bypass ICU. Post surgery Dr. Ahrendt told us there was a significant amount of tumor growth in the lower right quadrant of his abdomen. He didn't attempt any debulking. Rather, he advised the start of chemo as soon as Joey was healed. As we entered the recovery room, we could tell how happy Joey was to have his intestine back together.

Dr. Ahrendt advised him to let the nurse know if there was a lot of blood in either his stool or urine during the night. If his stool began to look tar-like in color or if he began to vomit any blood or tar colored liquid, he needed to push the call button. Again, he stressed the importance of starting chemo as soon as he was healed. After he left, I told Joey about the phone call from the Roswell oncologist. He said, "I would like to have my chemo here in Pitt."

Severe Blood Loss

That evening I wanted to stay with Joey, but he told me to go to the apartment and get some rest. In the middle of the night, I awoke with abdominal pain. I told myself it was my IBS because the nurse would call if anything were wrong with Joey.

The next morning we arrived at Joey's hospital room to find him having a blood transfusion. He had been up all night in the bathroom and felt too sick to call me, or the nurses, so he just sat on the toilet with his head down. He had gone to the bathroom several times, filling the bowl with blood. He knew he was bleeding, but he didn't realize how much danger he was in until he was too weak to care. By that time, he thought he was going to die.

When the morning nurse came in, she found him slumped over in the bathroom. His blood pressure was dangerously low. She got him into bed and paged the doctor. Joey told the doctor about the severe pain and bleeding. The doctor ordered blood work. The results indicated a major blood loss. He ordered an immediate transfusion of three units of blood at the floor's fastest rate. I sensed a lot of insecurity in Joey after his hemorrhage, something akin to post-traumatic stress disorder.

Unfortunately, Joey refused to complain about pain or any other symptoms. I found he would tell me his concerns quicker than he would his nurse or other health care providers. From that moment on, I spent my nights in his hospital room on a cot.

A few days after Joey stabilized, Alicia and Joe returned home. True to my word, I slept on a cot in Joey's hospital room for the next seven days. Again, Joey and I spent our time discussing life, religion, and sharing fond family memories. On good days we laughed together. On bad days we cried together. Some days I held his hand. Other days I kept my distance. But I was never physically far away. I was usually sitting in a chair in his room reading a book, watching TV, or answering emails and text messages from family and friends.

The support shown to Joey throughout his illness was amazing. There was a constant outpouring of gift cards, prayers, and donations. The genuine thoughtfulness of others was overwhelming. One of his former teachers sent him a card every week. Her tenacity and humor always cheered him up.

Joey told me he felt strange when people would give him gift cards and money because he felt he didn't deserve them. He decided he wanted to use the money to help others. We discussed various charity ideas. We thought about taking donations for cots so family members could sleep in the hospital room with their loved one. We would call it Caring With Cots. We spoke to the nurses on the floor. They loved the idea. If he beat his cancer, Joey wanted to buy apartments and rent them to patients and their families. He wanted to provide them with an affordable place to stay near the hospital. I promised him we would start a charity to help cancer patients and their families.

On July 19th, Joey was cleared for discharge. His father drove to Pittsburgh to meet us and we returned home to prepare for his upcoming chemotherapy.

The Military Calls

Joey had notified his commander of his terminal illness in March of 2012. Since that time, he hadn't heard from any one at the Army National Guard. Just a day after his intestinal hemorrhage, he received a call from one of his commanders. Joey asked me to call the commander back on his behalf because he was in no condition to speak with him.

I called the officer back and explained Joey's situation to him. He told me he needed a letter from Joey's doctor stating his current medical condition and prognosis. He gave me his full name and address. I told him I would have the letter sent to him as soon as possible. He told me the National Guard would be sending a care package to Joey at our home address. I thanked him for the thoughtfulness. Then, I contacted the surgeon's PA.

The next day, I had two copies of the surgeon's letter stating the extensive surgeries Joey had undergone, in addition to the pathology diagnosis of DSRCT. The letter stated Joey was no longer fit for active duty due to his medical condition, yet another one of Joey's dreams crushed by cancer. I decided not to show Joey the letter. I sent the letter by certified mail and Joey thanked me for taking care of the paper work.

3

As August Ends Aggressive Chemo Begins

"I keep dreaming of a future, a future with a long and healthy life, not lived in the shadow of cancer but in the light."

— Patrick Swayze

Like many people have, I had a family member who underwent chemo. For me, it was my father. Dad passed away in December of 2003, as a result of multiple myeloma. For him, chemo consisted of an outpatient IV infusion. He never got nauseous, never lost his hair, and never was hospitalized from a chemo-related side effect. I never realized how fortunate he was. I wish I could say the same for Joey.

Joey's chemo was entirely different from the start. He went through one of the most rigorous chemo regimens in existence. Each cycle lasted three days in the hospital as Joey was infused with four potent IV chemo drugs. Online I learned one of his drugs was nicknamed *The Red Death*. How was that for comforting words of encouragement? Joey never looked up his suspected cancer type or his chemo drugs. He felt the less he knew the better attitude he could maintain. I think he may have been right. Being a biology teacher, I felt the need to look everything up. I felt I had to know all about his situation so I could ask informed questions.

My research told me the drugs Joey would be taking were designed to kill many different types of cancer. In oncology circles, they were commonly used in the treatment of Ewing's Sarcoma and DSRCT. The treatment regimen is known as VACA and consists of consecutive infusions of Doxorubicin, Vincristine, Cytoxan, and Dactinomycin. He would also be given a drug called Mesna to help reduce bladder irritation caused by the chemo, along with lots of IV fluids to flush out the kidneys.

Joey's chemotherapy was hard on us. The anticipation of how sick he was going to get caused immeasurable anxiety. Joey looked so stoic and strong on the outside, but I could tell he was nervous and scared on the inside. He said, "It's hard to be calm, Mom, when you know they are going to pump your body full of poison."

By this time, all three of us were on anxiety medication. Prior to this cancer business, none of us were pill poppers. We seldom ever took Tylenol or Advil unless we had a fever. But, we knew the stress of the situation would get to us if we didn't face the reality of our anxieties. My irritable bowel had been acting up and I couldn't afford to lose any weight. Joe suffered from high blood pressure and angina, and he was having more bouts of chest pain. Joey had trouble sleeping, and his emotions were all over the place. His oncologist prescribed Xanax and Citalopram, drugs commonly used to treat anxiety and depression in cancer patients.

Joey's First Round

August 7, 2012, was the morning of Joey's first chemo treatment. We reported to the first floor of the Beckwith Center, located inside the Hillman Cancer Center. Joey checked in at the front desk. A nurse called him back to a sitting area where his port was accessed and his vitals taken. He was given an armband that officially admitted him to Shadyside Hospital. Before returning to us in the waiting room, he was told the hospital floor and room number where he would be receiving his treatment. We took the elevator to the second floor and Joey checked in at the oncologist's reception desk.

After a half hour wait, we were lead into an exam room by an oncology nurse. She told us the oncologist would be in shortly. As we waited, I could feel my heart beating wildly in my chest. I tried to remain calm, but all I could think about was my son undergoing such aggressive chemotherapy with no way out – no other options available to him. Just as I reached the peak of my anxiety, the door opened.

The oncologist smiled at us and shook our hands. He asked Joey how he was feeling. Then, he told us the UPMC pathologists believed Joey had DSRCT due to the EWSR1 chromosomal mutation present within his tumor. Based on their report, he wanted to start treating Joey with several well-known DSRCT chemo drugs. Since Joey had an elevated liver panel, the dosages of the chemo drugs would be adjusted to compensate.

He felt Joey's liver functions were elevated due to the cancer being inside the liver. If Joey's liver responded to the chemo, then he felt his treatment approach was on the right track. He reviewed all the possible side effects of the various chemo drugs, which included nausea, vomiting, hair loss, body aches, low blood counts, mouth sores, neutropenic fever, and infection. He told Joey he would be medicated for nausea and pain throughout, and after, his treatment.

Hearing all the possible side effects and need for pain medication made me extremely anxious, despite the Valium. I wished with all my heart Joey didn't have to go through this. I wanted to protect him, to shield him, and to spare him from any and all discomfort. I couldn't imagine how he was feeling or what he was thinking.

The oncologist excused himself, and a nurse came in. She told us she would lead us to Joey's hospital room. We left the cancer center and entered Shadyside Hospital through an attached bridge. She led us to an elevator that we took to the oncology floor. Here, the floor nurse took over. She had Joey change into a hospital gown, took his vitals, and told us his chemo was being prepared by the pharmacy.

I asked if I could stay the night on my cot. She smiled and said, "Certainly, family members often stay with their loved ones here." She showed us the Family Room located just around the corner from Joey's room. The refrigerator was filled with yogurts, individual assorted fruit juices, and milk. Patients or family members could place food in the refrigerator as long as the items were properly labeled.

An hour or so passed before the nurse came back to place a catheter in Joey's right arm for IV fluids. The fluids were started and he was given nausea medication. Exactly thirty minutes later, two nurses showed up with the four chemo drugs. Seeing the nurses gowned up was more than a little intimidating. One of the chemo agents was covered with a brown bag. The nurse seemed to be extra cautious handling it. A sign was placed on Joey's door warning of chemo exposure and proper handling of patient bodily fluids. The nurse verified Joey's name and patient number along with his assigned chemo medications.

His first chemo medication was injected into his accessed port over five minutes. Seeing that first drug entering his body was awful. I will never forget the look on Joey's face. I had all I could do not to cry. Over the course of two hours, we watched as the next two drugs were administered, followed by the last drug, Doxorubicin. The dose of Doxorubicin was reduced by fifty percent and given continuously over the next forty-eight hours.

Joey's nurse checked on him often to monitor any side effects. As the hours passed, Joey fell into his own private hell. He hardly spoke to us as he lay in the bed with his eyes closed. His body aches grew steadily and his stomach felt nauseous. He didn't eat or drink anything for fear of the possible repercussions.

Midway through the second day, his body aches were so severe that he asked me for more pain medication. I got the nurse and she increased his dosage. As the day progressed, Joey became increasingly agitated. He would snap at us if we asked him the simplest of questions. We stopped speaking to him, and let him speak to us when he felt like it.

His first round of chemo came to an end at 2PM on the third day. The oncologist on the floor prescribed Oxycodone for pain and Zofran for nausea. He told us to keep a close eye on Joey and to call him with any questions or concerns. Joey looked tired and worn. He took a wheelchair down to the front door of the hospital. Then, he slowly walked across the street with us to the hotel.

As soon as he entered the hotel room, he curled up in one of the beds and never moved for the rest of the day. All he did was take his medications and sleep. His personality was totally different. We couldn't ask him anything without being snapped at. Every spoken word was to tell us what we were doing wrong or how we were bothering him.

We tried our best to remember that this was the chemo talking and not Joey. The oncology nurses had warned us about chemo brain. They told us chemo brain affects chemo patients in different ways. Some patients start to forget things. Others become very irritable and lash out at those around them. Joe and I felt terrible. We hated seeing Joey this miserable.

Twenty-four hours after his chemo completion, I gave Joey a Neulasta injection to stimulate the bone marrow to make white blood cells. Unfortunately, the injection was known to cause body aches similar to that of the flu. Knowing I had to give Joey this injection when he was already feeling lousy made me feel despicable. Joey understood the need for the injection but this didn't make giving it any easier.

On August 10th, Joey started to feel better so we decided it was time to travel home. We had purchased a Roadtrek to transport Joey. The vehicle had an enclosed bathroom so we could travel without having to stop along the way. Joey felt awful the entire trip. He leaned against the front passenger side window with his eyes closed holding a bucket on his lap. We wanted to stop in Buffalo for the night, but he insisted we keep driving. We arrived home late that afternoon and Joey went right to bed. I knew he hadn't eaten or drank much of anything since he started his chemo, so I called Beth.

She told me it would be a good idea to start him on IV fluids. A few hours later, a home care company delivered the fluids, tubing, and IV pole to our door.

At first, Joey refused to let me hook him up. He told me he was sick of being tethered to a pole. I told him I understood, but he needed the fluids or he would end up back in the hospital from dehydration. Reluctantly, he agreed.

Post-Chemo Care

At the time of Joey's discharge, his oncology nurse gave us strict instructions regarding his post-chemo care. She told us to keep a close eye on him for uncontrolled nausea, sores in his mouth or throat, and fever of 100.5 degrees Fahrenheit or higher. Joey could not take any kind of medication that would mask a fever such as Advil, Tylenol, or Motrin. Also, I had to administer his Neulasta injection within the required time frame.

Should Joey spike a fever of 100.5 degrees Fahrenheit or higher, we had to report immediately to the nearest ER. She gave us written instructions to be followed by the ER doctors should such an event occur. The instructions stated that blood cultures were to be taken from his peripheral blood and his port. Then he should be placed on IV Vancomycin antibiotic within an hour of arrival.

She explained that neutropenic fevers, fevers that spike after chemo when white blood cells are low, usually occur between days seven and ten post-chemo. However, they can occur earlier. Not everyone undergoing chemo experiences neutropenic fever, but if they do the fevers must never be taken lightly as the body has little to no defense against invaders.

As you can imagine, I was driving Joey nuts taking his temperature. I was horrified he would spike a fever and I would lose him because I missed it. Just as I started to relax, the fever struck.

On August 15th, at 2AM, Joey knocked on our bedroom door with a bag in his hand. In the bag were his medications and the directions from the nurse in Pittsburgh. He told us we had to go to the ER because his temperature was 104 Fahrenheit. We jumped out of bed, got dressed, and headed to the local hospital. We were trying to stay calm, but I was terrified.

As soon as we arrived at the ER, I had Joey wait in the car. I told the receptionist at the check-in window the situation. I didn't want Joey exposed to anyone because he had a low WBC. She contacted the ER doctor on duty. The doctor came out and spoke to me. He gave me a mask for Joey and told me to bring him in to exam room three.

I went outside and gave Joey the mask. He put the mask on and we walked straight in to exam room three – an isolation room with a sliding glass door. The doctor had Joe and me gown up. Everyone coming into the exam room had to do the same. The nurse took Joey's temperature and it was 102. She started IV fluids. I gave her a list of all the medications Joey was on, along with the guidelines from the nurse in Pittsburgh. Blood was drawn for cultures and analysis, and a portable chest x-ray was taken. Within the hour, Joey was given IV Vancomycin and another antibiotic. Since this was our first experience with neutropenic fever we were worried, but relieved at how our local ER was handling the situation. I gave the ER doctor the number to Joey's oncologist in Pittsburgh. He called for additional procedural advice.

After five hours in the ER, Joey was transferred to an isolation room in the main hospital. He was kept on antibiotics and an anti-fungal was added due to sores discovered in his mouth. Thankfully, his blood cultures came back negative; however, he was severely neutropenic. The doctor told us Joey would remain in isolation until his fever subsided and his WBC count returned to a safe level.

Since we live in a small town, the hospital nurses are not used to dealing with patients in isolation. A couple of times, Joey had to remind a nurse or an aide to put their mask and gown on. Our greatest fear was Joey coming down with an infection and having no way to fight it. Beth had a discussion with the charge nurse and Joey never had to worry about the staff wearing the proper garments after that. It took four days for Joey's WBC count to return to safe levels.

On August 19th, Joey was discharged. He had one week to regain his strength before returning to Pittsburgh for a second round of chemo. Oh Lord, give him strength.

Second Round Scare

August 26th, we loaded the Roadtrek and drove to Buffalo. We decided to break our trip in to two, three-hour segments to make the drive easier on us. We arrived at our hotel in Pittsburgh around noon on August 27th.

On August 28th, we followed the same protocol for Joey's second round of chemo as we had for his first. Except, this time, the oncologist spoke with Joey about his neutropenic fever. He said he would normally reduce the chemo dosage after a patient experienced neutropenic fever. However, he was not going to do this in Joey's case. Instead, he wanted to give Joey the same treatment based on his normalized liver values. This meant his Doxorubicin would be increased. He told Joey his liver functions had returned to normal after the first round; therefore, he felt he was on the right treatment track. We were happy to hear the news. Joey said, "Whatever you decide, Doc."

After Joey's consultation, we returned to Shadyside Hospital for round two. Joey hardly ate or drank a thing while undergoing treatment. He knew the chemo would make his stomach nauseous and his body ache. Joe and I were upset this round, but not as anxious. Knowing what to expect eased some of our stress. Though I still spent a lot of time in prayer asking God to help Joey through his chemo and for the chemo to be successful. I knew we would be heartbroken if he went through all of this for nothing.

Joey seemed to handle round two much better than his first round. He was discharged on August 30th and the next morning we drove to Buffalo. We traveled the rest of the way home on September 1st.

At home, Joey settled into a routine of sleeping on and off. He would sit and visit at the kitchen table when he felt up to socializing. So he wouldn't get overtired, relatives and friends would stop by for limited visits. Additional limitations were put in place as well. No one could visit if sick or near anyone who was sick and hand sanitizer and masks were given to all visitors. This change of pace created some happy times for Joey. Unfortunately, his bliss was short lived.

On September 10th, Joey's mouth became intensely sore despite the use of saline washes. He spiked a neutropenic fever and we had to take him to the hospital. The ER doctor did the required blood cultures and Joey was given IV fluids and Vancomysin antibiotic; but this time Joey was experiencing extreme discomfort in his mouth and throat. The ER doctor decided to admit him to isolation in the ICU where he could receive higher doses of pain medication.

After Joey was transferred to the ICU, I met the hospitalist from hell. This doctor should not be allowed to practice medicine. The minute he met me, he asked me why Joey was sent to ICU. I explained Joey's history and gave him the phone number to the Pittsburgh oncologist. He told me he would call Joey's doctor. Two hours later, I asked him if he had called and he told me Joey's oncologist was out of town on vacation.

In the hours that followed, Joey took a turn for the worse. He became gravely ill. He could no longer talk, eat, or drink because his mouth was so sore. His tongue became cherry red and swollen. I had to give him a whiteboard with a washable marker to communicate with us. He wrote, "Please help me, Mom. My pain is 9 out of 10."

I asked to see the hospitalist several times, but he never came. I was so upset that I called Joey's oncologist in Pittsburgh. The clinical nurse told me Joey's oncologist was not on vacation and they didn't know Joey was in the hospital. The hospitalist had lied to me. I was furious. She told me to put the charge nurse on the line. The charge nurse spoke to her and then she gave the phone back to me. The clinical nurse told me Joey was suffering from a severe yeast infection. This type of infection is extremely painful. She told me the hospitalist needed to put Joey on IV Dyflucan and IV Acyclovir right away, and he would need Nystatin mouth rinse as soon as possible. She said she would notify Joey's oncologist. I thanked her for her time and compassion.

Meanwhile, the charge nurse paged the hospitalist and told him what the clinical nurse in Pittsburgh had said. Joe and I waited **hours** before any of the advised medications were given to Joey.

Later that night, Praise God, the same doctor Joey had when he had his first neutropenic fever came on duty. This doctor apologized to Joey for what he had been through and called the oncologist in Pittsburgh.

We experienced firsthand what a bad hospitalist can do. In ICU, our son suffered needlessly because his condition was allowed to go untreated. As a result, Joey had dropped to ninety-three pounds. He couldn't afford to lose any more weight.

The Loss of a Best Friend While in ICU

In June of 2011, while Joey was away at boot camp, his dog was diagnosed with throat cancer. The tumor was inoperable because it had wrapped around the major vessels in Shadow's neck. I knew the news would hit Joey hard. Every night I prayed Shadow would live long enough for Joey to see him again.

The Lord was kind enough to answer my prayer. When Joey returned from boot camp in August, Shadow was there to greet him. I told Joey the news. Disturbed, but optimistic, he told me not to worry because Shadow was a fighter. Well, Joey was right. Shadow was still going strong when Joey was diagnosed with cancer in March. I can remember Joey sitting down next to Shadow saying, "Looks like we both have cancer now, buddy. You don't go anywhere and I won't either."

Over the ensuing months, Shadow began to deteriorate. This was hard for us to watch because it seemed to foreshadow Joey's plight.

On September 8th, Joey and I took Shadow to the vet. The veterinarian told us he could give Shadow some steroids to help with his anemia, but we should consider "putting him down" in the near future. Joey understood and told me he wanted to be there with Shadow when the time came. He told me he wanted to bury Shadow on the side lawn underneath the flagpole where the American and Army flags are on display.

Two days later, Joey ended up in ICU with the neutropenic fever. One night, after visiting Joey, I returned home to find Shadow waiting for me in the garage. I sat on the step as he slowly walked over to me and rested his head on my lap. His eyes looked tired and cloudy. I hugged him and told him Joey was doing better. I said, "Joey will understand, Shadow, if you are tired and can't wait around for him." Smooching Shadow on his snout, I gently carried him up the steps into the kitchen. He lumbered across the floor and lay in his favorite spot by the laundry room door.

The next morning, Joe woke me up to tell me Shadow had passed away in his sleep. I held Shadow and cried. What a disastrous year this had been. How was I going to tell Joey he had lost his best friend while he was fighting for his life in ICU? I knew Joey would be heartbroken. As I drove to the hospital, I asked the Lord to help me say the right words. Joey was enduring enough hardship in his life.

Gathering my composure, I gowned up and entered his room. Immediately he asked, "What took you so long, Mama?" He looked tired, thin, and pale. I kissed his cheek and said, "I have some news to share with you." I explained how Shadow had come to me the night before, what I had said to him, and how his father had found him that morning. I said, "Shadow passed away peacefully, Joey."

Joey's eyes glassed over. I got up from the chair to hug him, but he waved me away. In a hoarse voice, he asked me to give him some time to himself. I quietly left the room and walked out to my car. The loss of Shadow, along with his current cancer battle, was just too overwhelming – why was he chosen for this path? I began to cry. I didn't cry for myself, I cried for Joey and the unfairness of his situation. Joey was such a kind-hearted soul, a good boy. Why was all this crap happening to him?

A half hour later, I returned to Joey's room. He sat gazing out the window. In a soft voice, he asked me where we had buried Shadow. I said, "Under the flagpole as you had requested." Joey looked down and said, "I just wish I had gotten a chance to say goodbye." Followed by, "I wonder if I will ever beat my cancer Mom?" A question we both had on our minds.

I told him Shadow was thirteen. In our years he was a very old man. He had lived a full and happy life followed by a peaceful death. Joey said, "Shadow fought hard, Mom, so will I."

Shadow and Joseph (Aug, 2011)

Joey's Strength is Revealed

Joey was moved from ICU to an isolation room on September 11th. On the morning of September 12th, a doctor came in to discuss the need for supplemental feedings with Joey. He told Joey he had ordered a special mixture of IV fluids to supplement his diet. He had to use less sugar and more proteins so Joey wouldn't develop a bacterial infection in his port. He suggested we talk to Joey about stopping his chemo treatments and enjoying the time he had left. We couldn't believe how hard two chemo treatments had hit our son.

Joey's eyes filled with tears when the doctor told him how sick he was. Joey was determined to continue his fight, so he began to force himself to drink two, eight ounce Ensure shakes three times a day. He amazed the doctors with his will power and determination because they knew the tremendous amount of pain he was experiencing in his mouth and throat.

Against all odds, Joey's efforts paid off. He began to build strength, his white blood cell count returned to normal, and his mouth sores began to clear. To everyone's amazement, Joey made a full recovery. We had witnessed a miracle.

Joey was discharged on September 15th with oral pain medication, IV fluids, antibiotics, anti-fungal, and antiviral medications. He was scheduled to have his third round of chemo in four days. I called the oncologist in Pitt and he pushed the chemo back to give Joey time to build up his strength. At this point, I was terrified. I knew Joey wanted to continue to fight, but could he survive another round of chemo?

Chemo Rounds Three through Five

After the close call we had with Joey at our local hospital, we decided to remain in Pittsburgh for twelve days after each of Joey's remaining chemo treatments. Since his body took such a hard hit with the thrush infection after round two, his oncologist decided to discontinue his Dactinomycin and reduce the dosage of his Doxorubicin and Cytoxan.

On September 25th, we were very apprehensive as Joey began his third round of chemo. We prayed Joey wouldn't get as sick as he had after round two. Our prayers were answered. Post-chemo, Joey was discharged on preventative antibiotics, anti-fungal, and antiviral medications. After this, Joey's treatments became easier.

On October 16th, Joey's forth cycle began. Now, he was able to walk around the hospital during his infusion. We would walk to the gift store where he would look through the various items, sometimes purchasing a gift for someone back home. On one occasion, he heard his cousin had been diagnosed with breast cancer so he bought her a glass angel and sent it to her. During treatments, we did everything according to 'Joey Time'...whatever he felt like doing, we did. Joe and I were there to support him any way we could.

After Joey's fifth chemo treatment, on November 9th, we thanked God Joey had made it this far. I had prayed every day for my son to be given the strength to carry on. Joey had endured numerous post-chemo complications and hospitalizations, yet he managed to put on some weight. He currently weighed ninety-seven pounds. There was no doubt in my heart Joey was an amazing young man because he had withstood pain and suffering beyond my comprehension.

When asked, I would tell people Joey had made it this far thanks to God's grace, his strong will to live, and their prayers. I told them I was able to maintain my sanity due to God's grace and Joey's courage. If Joey hadn't been as strong as he was, all of us would have fallen apart.

Scan Days

After chemo treatments in September and November, Joey had CT scans done to assess the cancer's growth. These days were tension filled as we waited to hear the news. The scan in September showed no evidence of disease – a real cause for celebration. However, the scan in November indicated some recurrent tumor growth in the abdomen.

I had heard DSRCT was more visible on PET scans, so I asked why a PET scan hadn't been done. The oncologist told me PET scans were very expensive and insurance companies didn't like to cover them as readily as CT scans. He would order a PET scan following Joey's sixth chemo treatment in December.

Thanksgiving

We considered ourselves blessed to be home for Thanksgiving. We kept the holiday simple because the flu was running rampant in Central New York. Joey and his father had gotten vaccinated just before Joey's fifth chemo treatment. I couldn't because I had had a reaction to the flu vaccine in the past. To be safe, I had only immediate family over for dinner.

I made Joey's favorite foods – turkey with stuffing, mashed potatoes, gravy, acorn squash, cranberry, snowflake rolls, and corn. For dessert I made chocolate pudding pie, pumpkin pie, and deep-dish apple pie. Joey ate well and we had a wonderful time together.

Once, during his chemo treatments, I asked Joey why he would stare at me so much. I would wake up some nights in his hospital room to find him looking over at me. He told me he was making memories, mental snapshots, to keep in case he didn't make it. He said he did the same with Alicia and Joe.

Now, on Thanksgiving, I was the one making memories. I kept watching Joey as I thought, "Will this be my last Thanksgiving with my son? Will next Thanksgiving and Christmas come without him?" Impossible. I prayed extra hard that night thanking God and the Blessed Mother for all they had done. I prayed the Lord would see fit to spare my son so he could have many more holidays with us.

The day after Thanksgiving, Joey asked if we could decorate for Christmas. He wanted some holiday cheer before he left for chemo in Pitt. We had a great day trimming the Christmas tree, hanging the wreath, and putting up the various decorations. Joe hung all the lights outside and positioned the inflatable lawn decorations. As soon as dusk arrived, the timer came on and all the outside Christmas lights and inflatable decorations came to life. I plugged in the Christmas tree in our living room and a big smile came across Joey's face. He said, "No one is ever too old to enjoy Christmas, Mom."

Round Six

If you had asked us if Joey could make it to his sixth chemo, we would have said his chances were slim. We had almost lost him so many times along the way. If we took the time to tally up all the days Joey spent in the hospital, it would total six months out of the past ten. Yet, he managed to fight and overcome all of the hardships he faced. Now, on December 4th, he was to begin his sixth treatment.

If his post-chemo PETCT came back with good news, he might be able to take a short break from chemo or continue on with a less intense regimen. Either way, Joey was looking forward to the end of the seventy-two hour chemo regimens. He hated being constantly tethered to an IV pole. By the third day he had an overwhelming desire to rip the IV out. I told him he did an amazing job at controlling his anxiety.

This would be the last treatment with Doxorubicin, one of the heavy hitters for his suspected cancer type. Doxorubicin builds up in a patient's body tissues and is stored for life. At high levels, it causes heart damage and other toxicities to the body, so only a certain amount can be given to an individual over their lifetime. Joey would reach his lifetime dose after the completion of this cycle. His heart was already showing evidence of damage done by the drug. His latest echocardiogram showed a reduction in left ventricular functioning.

Older cancer patients don't have to worry about the long-term chemo side effects as much as the younger cancer patients. In younger patients, oncologists have to think about their patient's quality of life down the road should they achieve remission or cure.

Joey's sixth treatment cycle went as expected and he was the happiest man alive when he was unhooked from the IV on December 6th. As per routine, we returned to our Pittsburgh apartment to await his neutropenic fever.

4

Aggressive Chemotherapy Fails

"You gain strength, courage and confidence by every experience in which you really stop to look fear in the face."

— Eleanor Roosevelt

Two days after Joey's chemo completion, he began to experience abdominal discomfort. I gave him a stool softener and mild laxative. Within cancer treatment circles, it is known that chemotherapy causes constipation. Joey never had an issue with this, up until this point. If anything, he was taking medication to slow his intestinal motility down.

Two days later, he still hadn't had a bowel movement. I wanted to call the doctor but he wouldn't let me. Soon, he was lying on the couch not speaking to us. We knew he was scared because we were scared. Late that afternoon, an oncology nurse called. She told me Joey had to come to the Hillman Cancer Center for a blood transfusion on December 13th. His recent blood work indicated a low RBC count. Joey promised he would tell the nurse about his constipation when he went for the transfusion.

After some discussion, we decided to check out of the apartment on December 12th and check in to the Marriott near the Hillman Cancer Center. This way we wouldn't have to travel in heavy morning traffic to his appointment. As fate would have it, we made it to the Marriott but not to his appointment on December 13th. Instead, we found ourselves in the Shadyside ER as the clock struck midnight.

At 11:30 that night, I woke up to the sound of Joey vomiting. I knocked on the bathroom door and asked if he was okay. He said, "No, Mom, come in and look at this. I think something is wrong." I opened the bathroom door to find Joey sitting on the floor with his head against the wall. He was pale and felt clammy to the touch. I glanced into the bowl. Joey had vomited fecal matter and blood. I woke Joe and asked him to stay with Joey as I called the oncologist.

The oncologist told me to take Joey to the Shadyside ER stat. Joe asked Joey if he could stand or if we should call an ambulance. Joey got to his feet, reached down, and picked up the trashcan. He carried the can saying, "I don't want an ambulance, Dad." We took the elevator down to the lobby and were able to catch a shuttle to the ER. Upon arrival, I told the receptionist the situation. She got a triage nurse and Joey was taken into one of the isolation rooms. There, he was quickly assessed, put on IV fluids, and an NG tube was ordered.

Joey asked me what an NG tube was. I told him an NG tube was a nasal gastric tube. A doctor or nurse would insert a small diameter plastic tube up one nostril and down the back of his throat into his stomach. The tube would drain the fluids from his stomach so he would stop vomiting. He asked me if the tube's placement would hurt. I told him it wouldn't feel pleasant but it would be over with fast, and he would feel a lot better.

I asked the nurse if she could spray the inside of his nose with something to numb it. She said she would ask. She came back with Lidocaine and gave Joey a few good squirts in his nostril and throat. She asked Joey if he wanted us to leave the room. He said, "Whatever they prefer." Joe opted to wait in the hall. I stayed in the room and held Joey's hand.

The nurse placed a bucket on Joey's lap in case he vomited from the procedure. She handed him a cup of water and asked him to sit up, tuck his chin to his chest, and lean forward. She began to insert the tip of the NG tube up Joey's nostril. Joey's eyes began to water. I could see the discomfort in his face. I told him to relax as he squeezed my hand. She asked Joey to swallow some water. As the tube made its way down the back of his throat, he started to gag and vomit into the bucket. Poor Joey – complication piled on top of complication. How much more could his body take? It was awful to watch him suffer like this.

As soon as the tube reached the stomach, it began to fill with dark green liquid. The nurse connected the exposed end of the tube to a plastic container on the wall. A steady stream of liquid flowed into the container until it was half full. Joey told me the procedure wasn't pleasant, but he felt much better. The intense nausea and pressure he had been feeling was gone.

After the tube placement, Joey had blood work, blood cultures, a chest x-ray, and a CT scan without contrast. The blood work confirmed Joey was neutropenic. The scan revealed a full blockage of the large intestine and a partial blockage of the small intestine. The doctor told us he couldn't give Joey an enema or any bowel medications due to his low white blood cell count. He would admit him and keep him on complete bowel rest. All of his oral medications would have to be switched to IV compliments.

It was 4AM before we got settled into a hospital room. The room had one recliner so Joe slept there. I sat next to Joey in his hospital bed. I knew my son wasn't feeling well because he laid his head on my shoulder. How my heart ached for him. I held his hand as I asked God to give him a break from all of this pain and suffering.

The oncology team visited around 8AM. They told Joey he would remain on antibiotics and complete bowel rest due to his low WBC count. Thus far, his blood cultures and port cultures were negative. However, they had to wait forty-eight hours before he was in the clear.

As the days passed, Joey's white blood cells returned to normal. Now that his body could defend itself, the surgeons wanted to introduce stool softeners and laxatives to help reduce the blockage. The oncologists didn't want to introduce anything. Evidently, the oncologists won because nothing was done.

Joey began to have slight cravings, so the doctors clamped off his NG tube and introduced clear liquids. He was told to take small sips. This went well. Then, he was advanced to semi-solids. He ate some pudding and ice cream. After a few days of semi-solids, he had some bowel relief. So, the oncology team felt it was safe to discharge him on a restricted diet and a mild bowel stimulant. The NG tube was removed and Joey was discharged at 4PM on December 18th.

Joey Suffers So

On the way to the Marriott, Joey told me he still didn't feel the best. By 8PM, he was vomiting green liquid again. Without hesitation, we took him back to the ER. I told the ER doctor Joey had been discharged four hours earlier. He paged an oncology surgeon and the surgeon remembered Joey. He ordered another abdominal CT scan.

The scan revealed a partial blockage in Joey's small intestine, the large intestine was clear. He ordered another NG tube placement. Joey endured the tube placement as I held his hand. This time he did better because he knew what to expect.

Joe and I were mentally, physically, and emotionally spent. Questions flew through our heads. What was causing the blockage? Was the cancer strangling his intestines? Why hadn't the oncologists and surgeons scanned his intestines before they had discharged him? We found ourselves on a roller coaster of emotions. God only knows how Joey was handling all of this. I'm sure, like us, he just wanted the complications to stop. Even if his mind was willing, his body could only take so much.

I found myself turning to my spiritual foundation to see me through the darkness. Closing my eyes, I asked Jesus to help us. I asked the Blessed Mother to help me endure as she endured her son's suffering. I prayed for a miracle...for God to spare Joey despite the odds he was up against.

At 11PM Joey was transferred to a hospital room. His father called home to update Alicia.

TPN through PICC or Port

The next morning, the surgeon came in. He told Joey he would need a PICC line (peripherally inserted central catheter) placed in his arm so he could receive TPN (total parenteral nutrition). At first, Joey declined the PICC because he was sick of surgical procedures. Who could blame him? The surgeon explained the dangers of administering TPN through the port such as an increased chance of systemic infection. The PICC line would be safer. If bacteria got into the PICC, the line would be pulled out and the infection treated. If the port got infected, it would require surgical removal. Joey decided to have the PICC.

As usual, he encountered complications. He never seemed to catch a break, so why should he now? The PICC nurse tried to place the PICC several times without success. She told us Joey would have to go to radiology to have the line inserted. We didn't see Joey for two and a half hours. When he came back, he was emotionally spent and physically exhausted. To make matters worse, there was no PICC in his arm.

The nurse said the doctor had tried three times to place the PICC but a blood clot had prevented the insertion. To our dismay, Joey would receive his TPN through his port. Joey was very upset. He tried to do the right thing and ended up going through hell for it. His upper arm was swollen, bruised, and sore. The three of us sat in silence. Nothing could be said that would make any one of us feel better. That night, the nurse hooked Joey's TPN to his port. As she did, I thought, "Please Lord, no systemic infections."

The Holiday Spirit

Christmas was approaching and Joey was starting to show signs of depression. He, his father, and I would walk the hospital hallways at night so Joey could get a change of scenery. As we walked, Joey would window shop outside the gift stores and look out the windows at the Christmas decorations displayed on the hospital grounds. Christmas music played over the hospital speakers and Joey would tell us when one of his favorite songs came on.

When the three of us sat in one of the lobby areas late at night I felt like we were in our own small world. Joey would talk about his childhood, politics, stocks, and ways to improve upon his medical equipment. Many times Joey and his Father would discuss physic's topics beyond my scope of understanding.

In moments like those, I just enjoyed seeing a father and son bonding. I could see how much they loved one another and how proud his father was of him. Joe would tell Joey several times a day he loved him. He would kiss him on the forehead and hug him. Knowing the uncertainty of Joey's future, all three of us cherished our time together.

I'll Be Home for Christmas

We planned on spending Christmas in the hospital. Joey was upset about it, but we told him Christmas would be Christmas no matter where we were, as long as we were together. Alicia said she would travel to Pittsburgh for Christmas to be with her little brother. She loved Joey so much – it wouldn't be Christmas without him.

On Friday, Dec. 21st, Dr. Bartlett came to see Joey. He told Joey he needed to undergo surgery after the New Year. He felt his current blockage was due to adhesions, from his prior surgical procedures, or cancer. As you can imagine, this really shook us up.

I asked Dr. Bartlett if Joey was strong enough for surgery. He believed Joey was. He told us he was sending Joey home for Christmas. We asked if it would be safe for Joey to leave the hospital in his current condition. He told us Joey would need TPN and IV fluids at home, but he should be fine. He told Joey not to eat anything solid, despite the temptation to do so. If he should start vomiting, he would have to call his office immediately. Based upon his condition, he would be advised to return to Pittsburgh or report to a nearby hospital.

Privately, I spoke with Dr. Bartlett in the hallway. He reassured me Joey would be able to handle the drive home. He told me he wanted Joey home for Christmas because it would be a bad situation if the cancer was causing the blockage. At that moment, I realized he was telling me this could be Joey's last Christmas. He told me he was sorry for all Joey had been through and what a great young man he was. I shook his hand and thanked him for all he had done.

To my amazement, I never got upset in front of him. Instead, I walked down the hall to the Ladies' Room, entered one of the stalls, closed the door, and cried. I couldn't imagine my life without Joey. I couldn't imagine a Christmas without Joey. Life was not supposed to happen this way. Parents are not supposed to outlive their children. Was this really going to happen to us?

By the time I had walked back to the hospital room, I had straightened myself out. Upon entering, Joey greeted me with a huge smile. He said, "I get to go home for Christmas, Beautiful." I hugged and kissed him. I didn't say a word to him about my conversation with Dr. Bartlett. Later that evening, in private, his Father and I held one another and cried.

Over the weekend, the nurses and support staff worked hard to coordinate Joey's discharge. They said they were having issues finding home care. The agency that had taken care of Joey in the past wasn't accepting patients until after the New Year. I became desperate, especially now that I knew this could be Joey's last Christmas. I spoke with a friend whose sister had connections. In no time, his sister was texting me. She told me she had left a message with a company she knew.

Meanwhile, I contacted an infusion nurse back home who cared for Joey after his HIPEC. I explained the situation to her. She told me she would take Joey on as her patient. I was elated. I told the charge nurse in Pittsburgh. She said we had one more issue to overcome before Joey could be discharged. I needed to have a nurse trained in TPN available to train me the day I arrived home.

It was 2PM on Christmas Eve, when I called another nurse I knew. I asked Mary Rose if she was familiar enough with TPN that she could train me. She said she would be able to train me under the supervision of an infusion nurse. I spoke with the floor caseworker and paperwork between Pittsburgh and New York was completed. Talk about a miracle – Joey was discharged at 4PM on Christmas Eve.

As I was making the nursing phone calls, Joe was across the street at the Marriott checking out. He packed the Roadtrek and drove to the main doors of the hospital to meet Joey and me. Joey was so excited. He would be home for Christmas.

Joey was still not feeling well, so he slept for most of the trip. We pulled in our driveway six hours later. Our house was ablaze with Christmas lights and inflatable lawn decorations. The sight made all three of us cheer. Joey was home for Christmas. The Lord had answered his prayers.

Mary Rose had left a family Christmas party to show me how to connect Joey to his TPN. We got Joey settled in and with the help of Jan, the infusion nurse, Mary Rose was able to show me how to prepare the pump and administer Joey's TPN. In no time, Joey was receiving his IV nutrition. I thanked both of them for taking time out of their holiday to help. We would have been spending Christmas in Pittsburgh if not for them.

Christmas Eve

My birthday happens to be Christmas Eve, and bringing Joey home for Christmas was the best gift ever. Joey had sent me the sweetest birthday text during our ride home. I can still remember his thoughtful words. He told me I was a beautiful mother and he was sorry his sickness had ruined my birthday. I deserved so much more and he hoped to get well enough to treat me to all the good things I deserved. He said I carried the weight of the world on my shoulders for him and his Dad and he was sorry. He loved me very much and always would.

I can tell you words like those are never forgotten when they are written to you on your birthday by your terminally ill son. My eyes filled with tears as I flashed back to my conversation with Dr. Bartlett. Would my Joey be with me to wish me a Happy Birthday next Christmas Eve? Would he be here to send me a text or would I be talking to him in a birthday prayer? I closed my eyes, took a deep breath in, and thanked God for getting us home for Christmas.

After Joey's TPN was connected, we sat around the kitchen table visiting with Alicia and Brandon. I can remember how good it felt to hear Joey laughing and to see him smiling. Joey was tired but happy.

Around midnight, we decided Joey should get some rest. Since he loved leaving the Christmas tree lit in the living room on Christmas Eve, it had become a family tradition. That night, Joey slept on the couch near the lighted tree. He told me he was really feeling the Christmas spirit.

Over the past few months, I had been ordering Christmas gifts online. I had them delivered to our house and my sister-in-law would hide them. I got up early Christmas morning and wrapped all the presents. I was exhausted, but determined to have Christmas as traditional as possible. Thankfully, Joey was so tired he never woke up when I placed the gifts under the tree. I loved the look on everyone's faces when they woke up to find presents waiting for them.

Since the flu was still an issue in our area, we watched Christmas mass on TV. After mass, Joe and I made our traditional Christmas dinner – stuffed turkey with all the fixings. Poor Joey, he couldn't eat a thing. He just sipped on water as we enjoyed the Christmas feast. I asked him on the drive home from Pittsburgh if he wanted me to skip the turkey dinner. He said, "It wouldn't be Christmas without turkey and all the fixings, Mom." That night, Joey admitted dinner was the roughest part of the day.

I couldn't imagine how he was feeling. He had been without food since Dec. 13th and would continue to be on a restricted diet for days to come. His surgery was scheduled for January 7th and he wouldn't be allowed to eat any solid food for weeks afterwards. This meant he would be without solid food for five to six weeks!

Christmas Eve (2012)

Ringing In the New Year

Joey's abdominal discomfort got worse after Christmas. He tried to do things with his friends, but he quickly tired from the pain. Knowing how sick he was, his friends did their best to accommodate him. They began to stop over for brief visits to play video games and watch movies.

On New Year's Eve Joey's best friend, Michael, asked him to go to the movies. Joey hadn't been out since his reversal surgery in July so he decided to go. I took this time to get the Roadtrek ready. I packed food, medical supplies, clothing, and Joey's paperwork. Joey hadn't been acting right and I wanted to be prepared to leave for Pittsburgh in a hurry. Three hours later Joey returned from the movie. He told me he didn't feel good at all. He felt some nausea and had pressure in his abdomen.

As the New Year's ball ushered in 2013, Joey began to vomit. Thank God the Roadtrek was ready to go. I woke his Father and we headed for Pittsburgh. On route, I contacted the surgeon and explained the situation. He told me to get to Pittsburgh as safely and as quickly as possible.

Meanwhile, he would call Passavant Hospital so the surgical resident would be expecting us. If Joey became too ill along the way, we would need to notify him and stop at either Upstate Medical Center or Buffalo Hospital.

Throughout the trip, Joey's pain intensified. We were petrified we would pass a hospital exit and he would turn critical in the middle of nowhere. Thankfully, that never happened.

At 7AM, just ten minutes from Passavant Hospital, Joey became violently ill. He started to vomit continuously. Green liquid spewed from his mouth and nose as his stomach heaved. All I could do was hold a bucket in front of him. Joe turned the emergency flashers on to help speed our way through the congested morning traffic. Joey kept asking, "How much longer Dad? How much further do we have to go?" His lips were ashen, his face pale, and he felt clammy to the touch.

I called the ER and told them our location. The nurse told me the resident was waiting for us. As soon as we arrived, I got a wheelchair and took Joey into the ER. Linda, a nurse Joey had before, wheeled him to an exam room in the back. She took his vitals, hooked him up to IV fluids, and told him she needed to place an NG tube. I held the cup of water and gave it to Joey as she slid the tube in his nose and down his throat. As soon as the tube entered his stomach, the attached canister filled with green fluid to its brim.

On route to Pittsburgh, the TPN pump had stopped working and its alarm never sounded, so Joey was dehydrated. I blamed myself for not checking the pump. The nurse tried to comfort me by saying I was only human and the alarm malfunctioned. She quickly pumped the IV fluids into Joey and told me he would feel better soon. After the NG tube placement, the surgical resident came in. She examined Joey, asked him several questions, and ordered blood work. Two hours later, Joey was stabilized and transferred to a room on 6 Main. All three of us were exhausted when we settled in to the room. Joey fell asleep right away. Joe and I set up our cots next to his bed and closed our eyes for some needed rest. Like all hospitals, nurses came in throughout the day to give Joey medications, check his vitals, and change his IVs. Joe and I had become pros at being able to sleep through these disruptions, so we were able to get a fair amount of rest despite the chaos.

God's Messenger

God works in funny ways. One day, Joey was telling me he was lonely. Just after he shared this, a very nice nurse's aide, around Joey's age, came into the room. She smiled and introduced herself. Joey introduced himself. The two of them exchanged small talk as she took Joey's vitals.

Over the next week, the two of them exchanged phone numbers and began texting. Then, she began to visit Joey on her days off or at the end of her shift. Joe and I were happy to see her spending time with Joey. Joey laughed and smiled when she was around. For the first time in months, he was happy. He had a relationship with someone other than family. He said, "God must have sent her to cheer me up."

Long Days of Waiting

The days in the hospital were long. Joey kept himself occupied by painting small figurines known as War Craft soldiers. He didn't play the game but he enjoyed painting the figurines.

Throughout the day, nurses and doctors would stop by to look at his figurines. They were shocked by his ability to paint such detail on hand-held figurines while on such high dosages of pain medication. This became an indication of the tolerance he was building up to these opiate drugs, a tolerance that increasingly concerned me.

Surgery Day

January 7th was finally upon us. Alicia had driven to Pittsburgh to be with Joey. At 7AM, Joey was taken to pre-op. Prior to his departure, he asked for some anxiety medication. He wasn't alone, all of us were anxious. Each of us gave him a hug and kiss before walking to the waiting room. The same waiting room we sat in for his HIPEC and reversal surgeries months earlier.

Joey's surgery took longer than anticipated, which caused us great apprehension and fear. Like before, I found myself visiting the chapel. Four hours had passed since the start of Joey's surgery when a volunteer came up to me. She said, "Dr. Bartlett would like to meet with the family in the adjacent conference room." My heart began to pound. The three of us went inside the conference room and sat down. We didn't wait long before Dr. Bartlett entered the room. He looked tired and frustrated.

He told us Joey had made it through the surgery and was in recovery. Unfortunately, the blockage was far worse than anticipated.

Joey's abdomen had a large amount of adhesions that resulted in several feet of intestine having to be removed. To make matters worse, the cancer had stopped responding to the chemo resulting in several areas of blocked intestine. These areas had to be removed as well. He decided against an ileostomy because he knew Joey hated his life with the last one. He inserted a gastric tube into Joey's stomach to vent the intestine should the cancer cause a future blockage. He told us Joey had less than five feet of small intestine left and the remaining intestine had cancer lesions on it. We were devastated.

Alicia asked Dr. Bartlett if Joey could survive with so little intestine. He said, "He can survive with a short gut, but it won't be easy for him to get the required nutrition. He will have to depend primarily on TPN, though he could still eat food by mouth."

Because his body was weak from the surgery, Joey was sent to ICU on a ventilator. We never asked Dr. Bartlett how long Joey had left. Instinctually he said, "Joey still has some time left. I am very sorry. Did he enjoy his Christmas at home?"

I remained composed until that moment. As I told him how much Joey had enjoyed being home, I began to cry. I hugged him and thanked him for allowing Joey the opportunity to be home for Christmas. Again, he told us how sorry he was. Alicia excused herself from the room. Joe, with tears in his eyes, shook Dr. Bartlett's hand. Dr. Bartlett said, "I wish I could have done more." Then, looking down, he left the room.

Absorbing the News

After a few minutes, Joe went to check on Alicia. I called my Mother to tell her the news. I couldn't bring myself to repeat the horrible news over and over again so I asked her to tell the rest of our family. I took several deep breaths and asked God for strength to get through this. I needed to accept, with his help, what I couldn't change.

Joe returned with Alicia. I spent time with her while Joe called his family. She was a mess. All her life she had been with Joey – she had never known life without him. She told me she couldn't bear the thought of losing him. She wanted him to see her pregnant and to hold her baby one day. She had so many memories she wanted to make with him...too many to list. I tried to comfort her as best I could, but I knew I couldn't take her pain away. I knew because nothing could take mine away.

I asked God why Joey had made it through six aggressive chemo treatments and numerous complications to have it all end this way. I simply couldn't understand. The whole thing felt surreal – how were we going to tell Joey?

Recovery & Realizations

On the way to ICU, the three of us agreed not to tell Joey about the surgery unless he asked. As we entered his room, we tried hard to mask our emotions. Joey was on the ventilator with his hands in mitts and his wrists tied down. He was hooked up to several monitors. As I walked up to him, he began to stir. I put my hand over his and told him I loved him. Alicia did the same. Joe stood to the side of the bed with his hand on Joey's forearm.

The ICU nurse told us he had his mid-line incision reopened during the surgery. So, a wound care nurse would be checking on him in the morning. He had spiked a post-operative fever of 104 Fahrenheit so she had placed ice bags under his armpits, in his groin area, and a large cooling pad underneath his body to help reduce the fever. His temperature was starting to go down.

Joey opened his eyes and tried to speak to me. The ventilator made it difficult but I could tell he was asking for pain relief. I said, "You want pain medication?" He nodded, yes. The nurse gave him an IV bolus and he fell back to sleep. We stayed with him for several hours, taking turns holding his hand.

Kim came on duty later that evening, but she was not assigned to Joey. She told me she would check on him. Around midnight, we went to the apartment to get some rest.

We were so upset over the news that none of us slept. By 6:30AM we were back in the ICU. Joey was awake and being weaned off the ventilator. We hated to watch this because the process looked so uncomfortable. He looked worn and tired – beaten down by cancer and all that accompanied it.

Gently, I gave him a hug saying, "I love you, Sunshine." He whispered, "I love you too Mom." Kim stopped to tell us he had a rough night with pain, but everything had been well managed. I stepped out in to the hallway with her. She gave me a hug and started to cry. I knew she had heard the results of the surgery. She said, "I'm so sorry." I said, "Me too."

After Joey stabilized, Joe and Alicia left to get breakfast. They planned on bringing some back for me. As soon as they left, Joey motioned for me to come closer. When he was a little boy, he would pull my face to his with both his hands, and look deep into my eyes. He did exactly that as he softly said, "What's wrong Mother? What are you scared of?" My eyes filled with tears as I replied, "Don't do this to me Joey. Please don't." He told me it would be okay, no matter what it was. He kissed me on the cheek and smiled at me. Again, he looked into my eyes and said, "Tell me about my surgery, Beautiful. It's okay, I need to know."

I proceeded to tell him the news. He listened intently, gazed down at his lap, and through tear-filled eyes said, "Is that all there is Mom? My candle will go out at twenty-one...my life will be over? Why, Mom, why?" I put me arms around him saying, "I don't know why." Then, we cried.

After a few minutes he sighed and said, "Look at it this way Mama, I will be with Grandpa. I will come to meet you when it's your time." I told him I should be the one coming to meet him. He was suppose to outlive me...it wasn't fair. I said, "My heart is breaking, Sunshine. I'm so sorry."

He proceeded to tell me how much he would miss me. How badly he wanted to be here to hold and play with Alicia's children. I said, "Only the good die young, Joey." He said, "I like that saying, Mom. It makes me feel better." I told him he would have a fast pass to Heaven because he was such a good person. God would certainly welcome him into his Kingdom. The rest of us would have to work hard at it.

Somehow, we managed to compose ourselves before Alicia and Joe returned. I sat next to his bed holding his hand. I never wanted to let go, as I thought how much I loved him.

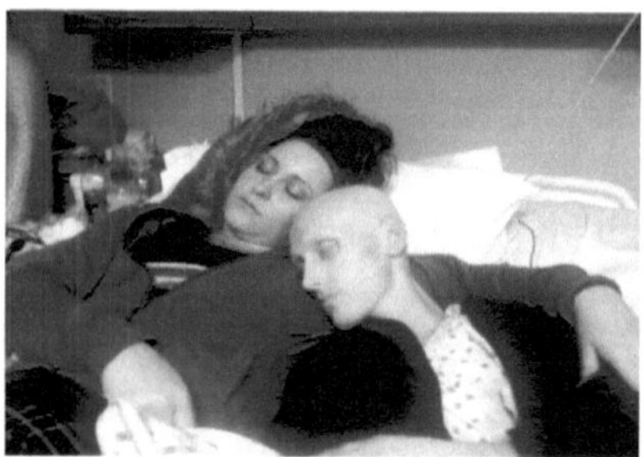

Joey and Alicia in ICU (2013)

Never Give Up, Never Surrender

Later that night, I told Joe and Alicia about the conversation I had with Joey. At first, Alicia was upset with me. But, I told her Joey had asked and I couldn't lie to him. The next morning, we made sure Alicia had some private time with Joey. Alicia said Joey spoke to her about the surgery and they both hugged one another as they cried. He told her he wanted to be around to see her pregnant and to meet her children. He said, "I always wanted to get married and have a family. Now, that doesn't look like it's going to happen." Alicia told him not to give up, to stay positive, because there were still options out there.

After three days in ICU, Joey was told he would be transferred to a room on 6 PAV. Since the hospital was being overrun with flu cases, Joey had to wait for a bed. At 10PM, Joey still hadn't been transferred so we decided to go back to the apartment to get some rest.

Around 4AM Joe woke up to his cell phone ringing. He answered and heard Joey's distorted voice. Joe tried to make sense out of his conversation but couldn't. I checked my cell phone. Joey had left me several messages as well. I had put my phone on vibrate while in the ICU; and hadn't turned the ringer back on before going to bed. I listened to his messages. He was desperately begging me to come help him with his pain. I was holding back tears as we got in the car and drove to the hospital.

Joey had been transferred to 6 PAV around midnight. We went directly to his room. His call button had fallen to the floor and he couldn't call the nurse. His pain medication had tapered off and he was hurting. He knew he had his cell phone so he tried calling the hospital switchboard but he was calling the wrong hospital. He called the same hospital several times asking them to send a nurse to his room. He was so out of it that he didn't realize he was calling Cranberry Hospital instead of Passavant.

He told us he had unhooked his finger monitor to see if a nurse would come. He thought the finger monitor was his heart monitor but it was just an oxygen concentration monitor. He told us a nurse checked on him at 2AM and gave him a pain bolus, but it had worn off.

Now, he wanted to see a pain doctor. Joey had developed a high tolerance to opioids and was on a good amount in ICU. His current dose was not working. Joe and I went to the nurse's station to explain the situation. A palliative pain doctor was contacted and Joey's pain was properly addressed.

A week later, Alicia and Joe returned home. Alicia had her new job to attend to and Joe had the family business, along with our house. I used this time to research Joey's options and make phone calls to different cancer hospitals to get their opinion. I contacted Sloan Kettering, Chicago Children's Hospital, Pittsburgh Children's Hospital, MD Anderson Cancer Center, and the National Institute of Health. Each hospital had an oncologist return my call. I collected valuable information from each of them.

As I pursued possible options, Joey's spirits started to improve. He began to walk around the hospital and to eat solid foods. Thankfully, the intestinal re-sectioning had healed without any complications. However, his midline incision had developed a few pockets of fluid. The wound nurse decided to remove the staples in those areas and apply wet to dry bandages. I would change the bandages twice a week. The surgeons wanted Joey ready for chemo so they ordered a wound vac to speed up the healing process.

The Walk

One evening, Joey and I went for a walk in the hospital. We ended up sitting on a small bench by the first floor gift shop. It was after midnight, so the entire floor was vacant. I said, "There must be a lot of angels in a hospital." He asked me why. I replied, "Because there are a lot of people in need of comfort. If I were an angel I'd be in a hospital." Joey smiled.

As we walked back to his room, he told me he enjoyed walking with me. He asked if I would go for more walks with him. "I would love to go for more walks with you, Joey. I will go as often as you like. No matter what time it is," I said with a smile. His interest in walking was evidence, to me, of his gain in strength.

The next night Joey asked me to go for another walk. This time we walked loops around the hospital floor. As he walked beside me, I pushed his IV pole. Joey told me he had something to discuss with me that he couldn't discuss with his sister or father. He wanted to plan his funeral.

He asked if there were Catholic cemeteries back home. I said, "Yes, a few. There is St. Peter's and Mount Olivet, the cemetery your Grandfather was buried in." He told me he wanted to select the cemetery and the location of his grave if he ever made it back home. He wanted to know where his final resting place would be. I told him, "Certainly, we can do that."

Then, he mentioned his calling hours. How would I ever get through that? Part of me wished he would have a private funeral so I wouldn't have to face the people. At that precise moment, God must have been listening because Joey told me how he and Alicia had said my calling hours would be hard on them but worth it. They would be proud of the lives I had touched as a teacher. Wow, did I feel selfish. Right then, I knew I would endure calling hours for him, despite my emotional state.

As we walked back to his room, I let out a sigh and looked down at the floor. Joey knew I was upset. He stopped, wrapped his arms around me, and said, "Thanks, Mom, for never leaving my side. You are the best Mom ever." Taking his hand, I gave him a kiss on the cheek saying, "I'm never going to stop praying for a cure."

That night, I prayed I would never have to carry out my son's wishes. I said a rosary with tears in my eyes and desperation in my heart. I asked Our Lady to send an angel to comfort my son.

Looking Forward

Early the next morning, I called Joe and told him about the conversation I had with Joey. After a moment of silence, he said, "Let's hope that day never comes." We decided not to tell Alicia about the conversation – it would just upset her.

Since the surgery, the palliative pain doctor was having a difficult time controlling Joey's pain. He was on high amounts of opioids but he was still alert and functioning.

One morning, as Joey was sleeping, a caseworker came to speak to me. She asked if I had a clear understanding of Joey's situation and wondered if I had looked into Palliative and Hospice Care at home. I told her I hadn't done so yet, but I would if Joey decided to return home. I said, "Joey and I both know the situation he is facing, and so does his sister and father. Joey is the one making the decisions. Our job is to support him, as long as he fully understands the ramifications." I told her I would speak with Joey to see what he wished to do. She said, "Please let me know."

Later that afternoon, I spoke with Joey about his future plans. He said, "I'm not ready to go home, sit around, and wait to die Mom." I shared the treatment options I had discussed with the other cancer centers, including a stem cell transplant. He asked me to contact Marissa because she had been cured of her aplastic anemia using stem cells. I sent Marissa a text. She told me to contact Dr. Karen Baird at the National Institute of Health. I called the NIH and spoke to Dr. Baird. She had an upcoming clinical trial using Natural Killer cells and stem cells. But Joey would have to have no evidence of disease to take part in the trial. I told her he had cancer lesions on his intestine and in his peritoneal cavity. She said, "I'm sorry but he wouldn't qualify for the clinical trial at this time. However, I will send you a kit to have his blood tested for stem cell matching in case he does become a candidate in the future."

I explained Joey's history to her and she recommended treatment with Irinotecan and Temazolamide or a single drug known as Pazopinib. In addition, she recommended I contact two surgeons –

Dr. Mike LaGualia at Sloan Kettering and Dr. Hayes-Jordan at MD Anderson. Dr. LaGualia was doing clinical trials using an antibody that targets a protein on the cell surface of DSRCT. Dr. Hayes-Jordan dealt extensively with DSRCT. I decided to call Dr. Hayes-Jordan first. Her surgical assistant recorded Joey's medical history and told me she would pass the information along.

Next, I called Dr. LaGualia at Sloan Kettering. I was able to talk to him directly. After explaining Joey's situation, he said Joey's cancer was too diffuse to treat using the antibody injections. Should his tumor become more concentrated, he could qualify for the treatment.

The next morning, a doctor from Chicago Children's Hospital spoke with me. He recommended Irinotecan and Temazolamide either together or separately. He said Etoposide and Ifosphamide didn't work as well.

Later that afternoon, the surgical assistant from MD Anderson called back. She asked if some of Joey's pathology could be sent to MD Anderson as soon as possible. She gave me the address and fax number of their pathology department. She asked if Joey was strong enough to travel to Texas for an immediate consultation with Dr. Hayes-Jordan and Dr. Anderson. I told her I would get back to her on that.

I shared the information I had collected with Joey. He decided to discuss the options with his UPMC oncologist. I called the oncologist and asked for a consultation regarding Joey's future treatment options. He said he would come to Joey's hospital room later in the week.

A few days later, the stem cell testing kit arrived at Passavant. The surgeon wrote a script so Joey could have his blood drawn and packaged according to the kit's directions. Our blood (Joe, Alicia, and mine) was drawn according to NIH orders as well. I took the completed NIH testing kit to UPS for shipping. We would be told the results in two weeks. If there were no matches for Joey within our family, his blood would be compared to the National Bone Marrow Registry.

The next day, one of Joey's former teachers called me. She had heard the news about Joey's illness and wanted to tell me her nephew was an oncologist at Pittsburgh Children's Hospital. She gave me his name and number. I thanked her for her concern and prayers. That afternoon I called her nephew, Dr. Scott Maurer.

Later that evening he called me back and gave me his opinion of Joey's situation. He said, "You have to find out what type of person Joey is in regards to his cancer. He is one of two types. The first type is tired of being sick and in the hospital. This type of person wants to go home and enjoy the time they have left. The second type is a fighter. A fighter can't stand sitting around knowing they have only a limited amount of time left. They want to keep trying to prolong their life with treatment. In either case, Joey shouldn't focus on a cure, but on prolonging his life with quality." I said, "I know my son's type. He is a fighter and he is looking to prolong his life with quality."

Dr. Maurer told me Joey could travel to MD Anderson as long as he was in the right mindset – prolongation, not cure. He explained his affiliation with Hospice. He was a pediatric palliative care doctor who worked with Hospice to control pain in children and young adults facing a terminal illness. He offered his services to Joey should he decide to return home. I learned a great deal from our candid conversation and I thanked him for his time.

Recently, I had been feeling a renewed sense of hope. I began to feel positive again about Joey's ability to beat this disease. After my discussion with Dr. Maurer, I was frightened. He had given me the reality check I needed. We had to keep ourselves on an even keel with this. We needed to stay as positive as possible given the reality of the situation we were facing. I knew I had to pray for Joey, for him to have the courage to face the truth and the strength to endure.

Later in the week, as promised, the UPMC oncologist stopped to see Joey. He told us he still suspected DSRCT despite the chemo not working as well as expected. He said DSRCT was known to become resistant to chemo. When this occurs, a new drug is introduced. He shared an article from Nature, March 2012, stating the discovery of the effectiveness of PARP inhibitors like Olaparib on Ewing's sarcoma (DSRCT). He wanted to put Joey into a clinical trial using Olaparib under his supervision. He told Joey to think about it. He would support whatever decision he made.

After he left, Joey told me he appreciated the recommendation; however, he wanted to go to MD Anderson. Since MD Anderson is the number one cancer center in the country, he hoped they had some form of targeted therapy. I told him we would support his decision.

5
Possibilitarian

"Become a possibilitarian. No matter how dark things seem to be or actually are, raise your sights and see possibilities - always see them, for they're always there."

— Norman Vincent Peale

January 29, 2013, was the MD Anderson consultation date. Joey was improving by the day and his pain was finally under control. I met with Dr. Bartlett's PA and told her Joey's wishes. She told me she would discuss our plans with the surgeon to be certain Joey would be ready for discharge in time. I filled out all the required hospital record and pathology requests and Joey signed them. The surgeon felt Joey would be discharged a few days prior to our due date in Texas – barring any complications.

Now, we had to figure out how to get Joey there. We couldn't expose him to colds and flu, so we decided to check into aviation medical transport. There are medical aviation services such as Angel Flights, Air Charity Network, and Mercy flights but we didn't have time to wait for insurance processing. I searched online for private jets out of Pittsburgh. I received several quotes by email and decided on a company called Skyward Aviation. They could fly us down and wait twenty-four hours for us.

The doctors and pain specialists at Passavant worked diligently to ensure Joey was well enough to leave for Texas on time. He was discharged on Fentanyl lollipops, Oxycodone, a wound vac, and TPN two days before his Texas consultation.

Welcome to Houston

On January 28th, we flew to Houston. We landed at 1PM and the weather was awful – high wind and heavy rain. We drove our rental car to our hotel at The Texas Medical Center. The center employs over 100,000 and sits on 1,345 acres so it feels like a city within a city. As we checked in, we were filled with excitement and hope.

The next morning the sun was out and temperatures were in the mid-fifties, a nice reprieve from the snow and cold of Pittsburgh. We took a hotel shuttle to MD Anderson's main entrance. MD Anderson was large, but everything was nicely labeled. We found the proper elevator and made our way to the Pediatric & Adolescent Clinic. Joey was exhausted by the time we got there, so we placed him in a wheelchair.

Joey's vitals were taken and we waited about an hour before being escorted into an exam room. I was so nervous waiting for the oncologist. My heart was racing. Finally, the door opened and a nurse practitioner entered. She introduced herself and asked Joey about his medical history – past surgeries, chemo, and pathology. She told us we would be meeting with Dr. Wells instead of Dr. Anderson.

Shortly thereafter, Dr. Wells entered the room. He told us he felt awkward because, up until ten minutes ago, he had known exactly how he was going to treat Joey. Now, he was no longer certain. Of course, this statement got our full attention. According to Dr. Wells, just ten minutes prior to our consultation an MD Anderson pathologist had called him. He told him he wasn't certain what type of cancer Joey had. Based upon the tests he had done so far, the tumor didn't appear to be DSRCT. He needed more time to conduct further testing.

At that moment, we were feeling a realm of emotions. We felt hope because the tumor may be curable if it wasn't DSRCT. We felt frustration because you can't effectively treat what you can't identify. We felt impatience as the tumor was growing and we couldn't act right away to stop it. All sorts of questions popped into my head. What if they couldn't figure out the type of cancer it was or its origin? What treatment options would Joey have then?

Dr. Wells decided it was best to use this investigative time wisely. He set Joey up with a variety of doctors. He established appointments with the oncology surgeon, a cancer psychiatrist, wound care nurse, radiologist, nutritionist, targeted therapy oncologist, GI liver specialist, and a pain management specialist. He also scheduled blood work and a PETCT. We knew these meetings and tests would take a week or more to do, so we called the pilots and told them to return to Pittsburgh.

Tests and More Tests

In the days that followed, Joey tired quickly due to his daily schedule of appointments. Each day, we would take a shuttle over to the cancer center and navigate our way to his various appointments. The radiologist told us radiation of the entire abdomen came with complication risks such as nausea, diarrhea, and intestinal blockage. Given Joey's current situation, she felt these complications would put him at higher risk. She told us radiation should be kept in his back pocket for now – to be used on smaller, targeted areas of cancer growth if it became necessary.

The liver specialist told Joey his bilirubin and liver enzymes were elevated, but his liver showed no evidence of cancer. He told us the elevated bilirubin and enzymes were most likely due to lipids in the TPN. So, he would adjust the fats in the TPN. He also prescribed a medication to absorb the excess bilirubin. Overall, he felt it was safe for Joey to undergo some type of chemotherapy.

Next, Joey had his consultation with the pain doctor. On a pain scale of zero to ten, ten being the worst pain one can tolerate, Joey said he was a three. The doctor was satisfied and no changes were made. Dr. Hayes-Jordan, the oncology surgeon, was concerned about his G-tube site. She felt it wasn't healing properly. So she ordered a PETCT and ultrasound of his abdomen to review the tube's placement and see how the tissue around the site looked.

The next day, we went to the Wound Clinic because Dr. Hayes-Jordan thought the wound vac could be removed. The wound nurse agreed. The vac was removed and the nurse showed me how to change and dress Joey's incision. From there, we reported to the psychiatrist to discuss how Joey was handling his diagnosis.

First, we met with the doctor as a family. Then she met with Joey privately. She gave Joey a prescription for Xanax and told him she would be available for future sessions. She told me the hospital conducted support meetings for parents and siblings.

Our final consultation was with the nutritionist regarding Joey's TPN. Joey had a test done to measure the amount of calories his body used at rest. During the test, he sat in bed with his head encased in a plastic helmet. He had to breathe normally for thirty minutes as a computer measured his oxygen and carbon dioxide levels. The results would determine the daily calories he needed in his TPN.

Angel Encounter

One morning, Joey and I were heading to his radiology tests at the Mays Clinic. We arrived at Clark Clinic and took a tram over to the Mays Clinic. On the tram, Joey sat to my right and an older lady sat to my left. As the tram was going along, the older lady smiled at me and said, “I bet there are a lot of angels here.” I replied, “Yes, I bet there are.” Then the tram stopped and we got off. I found it odd that she had said something to me similar to what I had said to Joey in Pittsburgh.

I proceeded to transfer Joey into a nearby wheelchair and head to radiology. After his x-ray, we took the tram back to Clark Clinic for another scheduled appointment at the Wound Clinic. The Wound Clinic was full when we arrived which meant a long wait.

As we were waiting, my phone rang. A friend back home was checking on us. I just ended my call when a middle-aged African American man dressed in jeans, a casual shirt, and a black leather coat walked up to Joey. He asked if he was Christian. Joey replied, “Yes." He asked if he could pray with him. Joey said, “Sure.” He put his right hand on Joey’s right shoulder. He closed his eyes, looked up, and said a prayer out loud. He used a normal, indoor, voice. He asked Jesus to heal Joey’s liver, to cleanse every cell in his body of cancer, and to bring Joey strength. He praised the Lord for his great mercy. After he was done praying, he looked down and said, “When you leave here everything will be okay.” He repeated the statement waiting for my son to acknowledge his words. Joey nodded.

The man never acknowledged me until I spoke up and thanked him for praying with my son. He nodded, turned away, and walked out of the waiting room. Oddly, no one else in the room seemed to pay attention to him as he was praying for Joey. The man next to me continued to read his paper and others continued to watch the television.

After the man left, I asked Joey what he thought about the whole experience. He told me he felt the man was an angel sent to him with a message. The message was simple – whether he made it through cancer or not, he was going to be okay. We looked for the man every time we came to the clinic after that but we never saw him again.

As we discussed the encounter more, we couldn’t get over the man praying for Joey’s liver to be healed. Joey’s liver was bad at the time, but we hadn’t spoken about it at the clinic. I wondered about the events of that day for months afterwards. Would Joey achieve remission or would he pass away?

Many times I found myself thinking how hard all this must be on Joey. I could see the stress in him. I could feel his sadness when I hugged him. He once said, “I wish I knew if I was living or dying because I hate to make plans in my head that will never come true.” I told him I couldn’t imagine being in his shoes. The constant stress of not knowing your fate had to be overwhelming. At such a young age, he was facing his mortality.

My heart ached for him because I knew most people his age were going out and having a good time while he spent his days trying to keep food in, medicine down, and his mind off dying. To get up and make breakfast was a chore, nothing came easy to him, and everything had a price. Just trying to follow a conversation was exhausting for him. Many times he said, "I have a young mind trapped inside an old man's body." Just looking at him, anyone could see the price he paid for fighting this disease. People would stare at him with pity.

As his Mother, this broke my heart. I wanted him to have better quality of life than this. I wanted him to have time to share his many gifts with others in this world.

Bed Bugs in Houston

After being in Houston for two weeks, we decided to rent a corporate apartment. I found a two bedroom, one bathroom apartment about ten minutes from the cancer center. We decided to take it, as a monthly rental, because it was cheaper than the hotel.

We moved in and everything appeared to be fine. One bedroom had both a twin and a queen bed while the other bedroom had a king bed. Both bedrooms were adjacent to the bathroom. Joe and I stayed in the same bedroom as Joey. We slept on the queen and he slept on the twin. This enabled me to keep an eye on his TPN and other medical needs throughout the night.

One weekend Alicia and Brandon decided to come down to visit. She and Brandon slept in the second bedroom, which hadn't been used until then. The next morning, Alicia told me she had been bitten in several spots. Brandon woke up and saw a bug on her pillow and killed it. He put the bug in a plastic bag and looked it up online. It was a bed bug. I called management and he came over. Alicia showed him the bites and the bug in the bag. The man told us he would move us to another apartment but it would take a day to get the other place in order.

Alicia moved the luggage out of the bedroom and washed all of their clothing. The manager sprayed Brandon's luggage. The next day, Brandon flew home. Alicia stayed for an additional two days to help me care for Joey.

The next morning, Alicia helped me pack our belongings and load the rental car. I drove to the other apartment across town while Alicia stayed with Joey. The apartment complex was located in a rough neighborhood. As soon as I entered the living room I could smell a musty odor, akin to wet laundry. I opened several windows to let some fresh air in. The kitchen and bathroom looked clean, so I decided to give the apartment a try. It took me three trips to bring everything over from the original apartment. Alicia and Joey came with me on the final trip.

As soon as Alicia entered the apartment, she told me to call the manager about the smell. He told me the rugs had just been cleaned and were still damp. I didn't want to be too unpleasant, so I decided to see how the night went. Alicia and I set up house as Joey slept on the couch. After watching a movie, we decided to go to bed.

We hadn't been asleep for long when Alicia got bit. She woke me and I checked the bed she had been sleeping in. I found dead larvae under the fitted sheet, within the stitching of the mattress. Alicia put some of the larvae into a plastic bag. Since it was early morning, we decided not to call the manager. I moved Joey to the couch and we slept on the living room floor.

At 8AM, I called the manager. He didn't believe me and accused my daughter of bringing the bugs with her from New York. I demanded that he come over. I showed him the larvae in the mattress. He told me they were not bed bugs but some kind of beetle. I told him I didn't care what kind of bug they were, we shouldn't be sleeping in infested beds. Alicia was disgusted and showed him the new bites on her shoulder.

At this point, I had to leave with Joey for a doctor's appointment. I knew we couldn't stay there for another night. Alicia packed up our belongings, while I was at the respiratory doctor with Joey. She called her father and told him what had happened. Joe called the manager and exchanged words about the bed bugs and "beetles". The manager said he would refund our monthly rent, but *WE* couldn't stay at any of his corporate apartments in Houston.

After Joey's respiratory test, I loaded up the car with Alicia's help. We drove to the Marriott and checked in. Alicia and I walked Joey up to our room. Not wanting to take the chance of bringing bed bugs into the Marriott, I had placed all of our clothing in plastic garbage bags in the trunk of the car. While Alicia stayed with Joey, I drove to a pest control business located in downtown Houston so I could show them the larvae in the sandwich bag. The pest control official looked at the larvae and told me they were bed bugs. He sold me some spray and told me what had to be done with my laundry and suitcases. I had him write down a signed statement about the type of larvae and he gave me his business card. I kept them as evidence should the apartment manager neglect to refund us.

In the parking lot, I sprayed our suitcases. Then, I washed all our clothing in hot water with detergent and bleach. I finished the laundry at 2AM – overtired and fed up with bed bugs and moving. As advised, I placed all our clean clothing into large zip lock bags before bringing them up to our hotel room.

We stayed a week at the Marriott. Then, I was able to book a room at the Rotary House located across the street from MD Anderson and attached by an enclosed walkway.

New Treatment Decided

On February 12th we meant Dr. Wells for the second time. He reviewed the latest pathology results and all of Joey's tests with us. He told us the pathologist didn't believe the tumor was DSRCT, despite the EWSR1 rearrangement, because the tumor was lacking a WT1 fusion transcript commonly found in combination with the EWSR1 rearrangement. The pathologist believed the tumor was either an adenocarcinoma of unknown origin or a sex chord tumor. In the final report, the pathologist indicated Joey's cancer was a very difficult case to diagnose. Several of the best pathologists in the country had trouble with the tumor's identification.

Dr. Wells told us sex chord tumors were rare and very little was known about treating them. Frustration ran rampant in our circle. Based upon the pathology report, he felt the selected chemotherapy agent(s) should cover both types of cancer. He decided to try BEP (Bleomyocin, Etoposide, and Cisplatin).

Since Joey was still weak from his past surgery, Dr. Wells felt it was best to hospitalize Joey for his first round. He ended the consultation by telling Joey his PETCT showed tumor stabilization since his surgery in January, a tiny ray of sunshine in an otherwise relentless storm.

Joey's BEP was scheduled for February 25th. Not knowing how this chemo would affect Joey, we were a bundle of nerves. Since Joey had endured such aggressive chemo in the past, we prayed BEP would be a walk in the park.

Since Dr. Wells was a pediatric oncologist, Joey was admitted to the pediatric oncology floor. This was hard on us because we saw many little ones undergoing chemotherapy. I always felt empathy for the parents of the little toddlers walking around hooked up to chemo. One parent told me she felt worse for me because Joey knew everything that was happening to him and would always remember it. She told me her child wouldn't have memories of his treatments. I hadn't thought of it like that. Again, perspective makes all the difference.

The BEP was given to Joey through IV three hours a day for five days. Joey was on nausea medication and wasn't eating much just in case. The treatment caused an increase in Joey's abdominal pain; so his pain medications were increased. Prior to his discharge on March 1st, the pain doctor switched his Oxycodone to Oxycontin. I thought Joey should try the medication for a day before leaving the hospital, but he was eager to get out.

Unexpected Chemo Crash

By morning, Joey was experiencing intense abdominal pain and vomiting. He threw up three times in less than an hour. He couldn't keep any of his medications down. I called Dr. Wells. He told me to bring Joey to the ER.

At the ER, Joey was taken in rather quickly because of the nausea and pain. He was given IV fluids and nausea medication. But it took over three hours to get his pain medication. By this time, his pain was an eight out of ten. We watched helplessly as he held his abdomen.

By 6PM Joey was stabilized and transferred to the pediatric oncology floor. He never left the hospital for the next six weeks as he endured numerous complications. Any of which could end his life.

VRE

Upon arrival to his room on the pediatric floor, Joey was placed under isolation because he tested positive for VRE, Vancomycin Resistant Enterococcus bacteria. The bacteria were colonizing his intestine, but he wasn't actively spreading it.

Anyone entering his room had to wear a mask, gloves, and a gown. Joe and I wore them when we were in the room, even when we were sleeping. If we left the room, we had to remove them and throw them out in a designated container. New masks, gowns, and gloves would be put on when we reentered the room. If Joey left the room, he had to wear a mask, gown, and gloves.

The first few nights Joe and I slept very little due to the nurses coming in and out of the room. By the third night, we had become accustomed to their schedule. Daily between 8AM and 10AM the oncology team made their rounds. They would give us an update on Joey's progress. His nausea was under control but his pain was still high despite the use of IV Dilaudid and Oxycodone.

The forth day in the hospital, I noticed an area around Joey's G-tube becoming pink and swollen. He told me his pain was highest in that area. I informed his nurse and she paged the surgeon.

Joey had been suffering from fevers on and off and his white blood cell count was below normal, so any area of discoloration and inflammation had to be investigated. The surgeon decided the area should be cultured for bacterial growth, along with his peripheral blood and port. We would be told the results within forty-eight hours. Meanwhile, Joey was given a couple different antibiotics. Waiting for the results was the longest forty-eight hours of our lives. We knew Joey had no ability to defend himself should he have an infection.

The Talk

Within twelve hours, our worst fear was confirmed. All of Joey's cultures grew bacterial colonies. He had developed a systemic infection. The G-tube had become so swollen and painful that the oncologist had to call chronic pain services.

By the evening of the fifth day, Joey began to crash on us. His body was weak and struggling. He looked terribly pale and gaunt. With tears in his eyes, he told us how sorry he was for his loss of bowel control. I told him it wasn't his fault. I explained to him it was his body's way of reacting to the infection. I held his hand saying, "We love you Joey – hang in there Sunshine. God is with you."

Scared beyond belief, I told Joe and Joey I needed to use the restroom. In the hallway, I found a vacant area and called Alicia. I told her Joey wasn't doing well. I didn't know if he would make it. She told me to call her if his condition worsened. She would take the first available flight to Houston. I reassured her I would. I ended my call, took a deep breath in, and wondered what was in store.

On my way back to Joey's room the pain doctor asked if she could speak with me. She escorted me into an empty room. In a compassionate and sincere voice she asked me if Joey had discussed the possibility of returning home with Hospice. She told me how sick he was and she wasn't certain he was going to make it through the infection. If he did make it, his body wouldn't be able to handle another chemo treatment.

I told her, with tears in my eyes, Joey was aware of the treatment risks and he knew he might not make it back home should he become too ill to travel. I told her we promised Joey that we would support his decisions. If he decided to fight, we would fight. If he decided to go home, we would go home. Joey didn't want to wait around for death to come. Instead, he wanted to fight to the best of his ability. If there was a chance of being put into remission, Joey wanted to go for it.

I said, "Joey has already shared his last wishes with me." She responded, " I am glad you discussed his end of life with him because many families wait until the last minute." She told me Joey was an amazing young man and she could tell we were a close family.

I dried my eyes, composed myself, and left the room. I was expecting this conversation at some point. I had experienced a similar talk twice before. The first happened when Joey was sick from the thrush infection after his second chemo, and the second occurred after his intestinal re-sectioning in Pittsburgh. Each time I felt the same flood of emotion. After all, no parent is comfortable discussing the death of their child.

When I arrived back at the room, Joey was sleeping comfortably. I took Joe aside and told him about the conversation I had with the pain doctor. His eyes filled with tears. He suggested we go to the chapel to say a prayer for Joey. In the chapel, I asked the Lord for grace to accept his will. I didn't want Joey to suffer needlessly. If Joey wasn't going to get better, I wanted him to fall asleep peacefully. He deserved better than the pain and suffering he was enduring day in and day out.

The Blessing

Joey was still sleeping when we returned from the chapel. The nurse told us his vitals were stable. I asked if a priest could come to bless him. She told me that could be arranged. Later that evening, a priest came by. He introduced himself and asked Joey if he would like to receive the Blessing of the Sick. Joey said, "I would like that very much Father." Joey had the Blessing of the Sick several times since his initial diagnosis, and it always made him feel better. The priest blessed Joey as we placed our hands on him.

The next day, Joey continued to apologize to us for being grumpy and not having bowel control. We had all we could do not to cry in front of him. We were amazed at his concern for others over himself.

That night, my mind was racing with thoughts of Joey. I couldn't fall asleep so I decided to write my emotions down. The words just seemed to flow effortlessly from my mind to my pen.

<u>*I Cried a Tear Today*</u>

I cried a tear today as I got down on my knees and prayed
I asked the Lord to help my son, I asked the Lord what must be done
I asked him to hold my son's hand and to leave his footprints in the sand.

I cried a tear today as I got down on my knees and prayed
I asked Angels to sing songs of grace that would bring a smile to my son's face
I asked them to stay by his side, to always be his light and guide.

I cried a tear today as I got down on my knees and prayed
I asked Mary to speak to her son, so a miracle could be done
I asked her to bring relief from the pain, so my son felt good again.

I cried a tear today as I got down on my knees and prayed
I thought about what my son had said as he spoke to me from his hospital bed
My son told me, "God has a plan, a plan for each and every man."

The next morning, Joey's doctors ordered an ultrasound of his G-tube, a scan of his abdomen, and an EKG. The EKG was done at his bedside. Joey's prolonged QT wave had gotten worse. The doctor told us certain medications can enhance the prolongation and cause the heart to have a problem with proper rhythm, so Joey's medications had to be checked.

Next, Joey went to radiology for his scan and ultrasound. Both tests were being done to check for an abscess, tumor growth, and possible blockage. We walked beside his stretcher as he was transported to the radiology floor. He was so ill that he was in and out of consciousness. Every so often, he would open his eyes and say, "Hello beautiful". I held his hand and kissed his forehead. The tests took about an hour.

Shortly after returning to his room, the oncologist came to share the test results. The ultrasound showed no abscess in or around the G-tube site. The scan revealed no advancement of the cancer since his last scan and no apparent blockages in the abdomen. However, the scan did reveal a large blood clot in Joey's Inferior Vena Cava, a large vein leading to the heart, just above the kidneys.

A vascular surgeon came to see Joey. He drew a picture of Joey's lower body and showed him where the clot was. He said, "This is a very dangerous situation. If the clot breaks free it could travel into your lungs or heart." Joey needed the prompt placement of an IVC filter. He dreaded having another procedure, but he knew it was necessary.

Dr. Wells also told Joey a team of doctors from Infectious Control would be coming to see him. They would be making further recommendations to address his underlying infection.

The next morning, Joey was very anxious. He was dreading the filter procedure because he had undergone a difficult IVC removal in Pittsburgh. I asked the nurse if any medication could be given to him.

She checked with his doctor and came back with a sedative. Just before he was transported to the procedure, Joe and I gave him a kiss.

Joey was gone an hour. Afterwards, he told us he could feel some of the procedure but it wasn't that bad. According to him, they fed the filter through a vein in his neck as they watched the process on an overhead monitor. Again, his body was covered in a plastic sheet to create a sterile field.

Joe and I were relieved to know the procedure went well. The vascular surgeon told us the filter would never be taken out. This meant Joey would be on blood thinner for the rest of his life. Joey was not pleased, but he understood the surgeon's rational. I thanked the Lord for getting Joey over yet another obstacle.

That night, Infection Control team took over Joey's care. He was placed on three strong IV antibiotics and nausea medication. Within a week, the team was able to kill the underlying infection. We were so happy to see our son smiling again. I knew we had received another miracle.

The Power of Prayer

Some nights in the hospital I would hold Joey's hand and tell him stories about his childhood. If he felt up to it, he would share stories with me. Every night ended with us saying, "I love you." Some days, Joey would ask for hugs several times throughout the day. We would hug him and tell him how proud we were of him.

By week three, around March 17th, Joey was still fighting his way out of the danger zone. The oncologists struggled to keep his red blood cells and platelets at normal levels. He underwent five blood transfusions and three platelet transfusions in a week's time. To everyone's discouragement, his G-tube site refused to clear up. The oncologist decided to do repeat cultures. To our dismay, the same bacterial infection had returned in Joey's port and G-tube site.

The Infectious Control team recommended the prompt removal of Joey's port because the bacteria were resistant to many antibiotics. Joey would need his port removed and a PICC line placed in one of his arms. I told the surgeon about the trouble Joey experienced in Pittsburgh when doctors tried to insert a PICC.

That evening, Joey had an ultrasound done on his upper chest to select an arm for PICC placement. The right arm was selected because the left had a blood clot blocking several veins. The surgeon didn't want to delay, so the port removal was scheduled for the next morning.

Unfortunately, Joe had flown home two days prior to the surgeon's announcement because we had been told Joey's port wouldn't be operated on. He was very upset. He didn't want me there alone when Joey was in surgery. I assured him I would be fine.

Early the next morning, I gave Joey his usual hug and kiss before reporting to the surgical waiting room. In the waiting room, I prayed for a successful surgery. I figured the Lord was sick of hearing from me by now. Maybe he would say, "Cure that lady's kid." At least that was what I was hoping for.

The surgery took two hours. Post surgery, the surgeon told me the port was compromised and was actually breaking through Joey's skin. The surface exposure made the site highly susceptible to infection so the port had to be replaced even if it wasn't infected. She told me the PICC line was placed in his upper right arm without complication. I was relieved and called Joe to share the good news.

When I saw Joey in recovery, he was semi-conscious and stable. The nurse told me he had been given a unit of blood during the procedure and he would receive another unit when he returned to the floor.

As soon as I touched Joey's hand, he opened his eyes and asked me how the surgery went. I shared the good news. He closed his eyes and grinned. As I looked down at him, I couldn't help but wonder if he was going to make it through all of this. Sometimes I felt like I was just kidding myself, but I couldn't bear the thought of losing him. I couldn't imagine not being able to see him and talk with him. I would miss him too much to fathom – a void in my life and a hole forever in my heart. We remained in recovery for an hour before returning to the floor.

Over the next few days, the Infectious Control team continued to monitor Joey. His blood was cultured daily because they needed three consecutive negative results in order to classify the infection as terminated. Four days after the surgery we were told the port removal and antibiotics were successful. The surgeon and oncologist were happy because they didn't expected Joey to recover. Again, we experienced the power of prayer and the grace of God.

Lego-Therapy

Joey had been dealing with severe neutropenia and abdominal pain day in and day out for twenty-one days. Never before had it taken so long for his bone marrow to recover. His pain medications and dosages were altered on a daily basis in an attempt to find the right balance. The chronic pain team couldn't understand how Joey's body was able to process such high dosages of opiates so quickly. They began to wonder if they would ever get his pain under control.

They refused to increase his continual rat out of fear of causing respiratory distress. At one point, they told him the pain medication itself could be causing the increased pain – a response that isn't fully understood. After five weeks of his pain hovering between a seven and an eight, the pain team decided to try a higher continuous rate of Fentanyl by PCA. They also added a self-bolus every eight minutes and a nurse bolus every hour. A few days after implementation, Joey's pain dropped to a five. He was so happy. He never thought his pain would be at a tolerable level again. He said, "It feels so good, Mom. Being in constant pain is physically and mentally exhausting."

I started to buy Joey Lego sets to keep his mind busy. He loved them as a child and I knew the construction would keep his mind off his pain. Despite his discomfort, Joey would get up and work on his Lego Star War sets. He would sit in the chair constructing for an hour or more. The doctors were amazed at how fast he would put the various designs together. His favorites were R2D2 and the Death Star. He received several compliments from doctors, nurses, and staff on his collection.

After six weeks in the hospital, he had completed twenty-two Lego models. I loved to see him enjoying himself. We used to say he was doing "Lego Therapy".

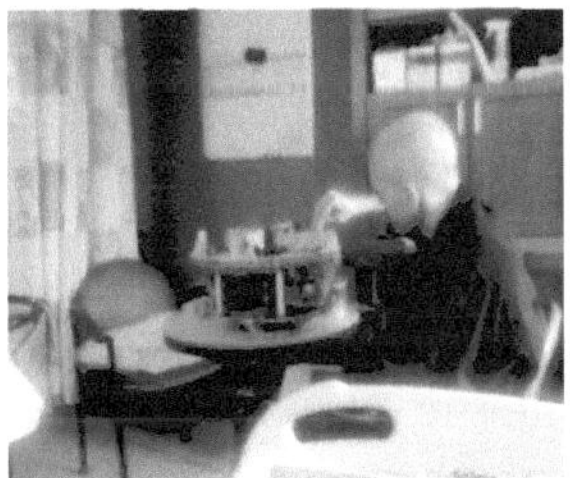

Joey building the Death Star

Medical & Honorable Discharge

While in Texas, Joey heard from the National Guard. This time they wanted him to sign paperwork stating he failed to complete his contract. This was not acceptable. Joey completed boot camp and he was heading to OCS when he was diagnosed with cancer. Signing the form could impact future employment for the government and other agencies. After reading this, Joey refused to sign.

I contacted his commander. He told me the paperwork didn't reflect a dishonorable discharge. I told him Joey was not going to sign any form accusing him of failure to complete his contract. The signing of such would put him in the same category as someone who never attended or completed training. I told the sergeant Joey deserved the proper paperwork and discharge.

I gathered Joey's medical records and Joe flew home with them. He hand delivered the records to the Army National Guard Office. Several weeks passed before I received a phone call from another National Guard commander. He asked me a series of questions. I told him about the letter written on Joey's behalf when he had his surgery in July. He said he wasn't aware of the letter but the military doctors had reviewed Joey's medical records. Joey would be receiving an honorable discharge and a medical discharge. I thanked him for his time.

Several weeks passed and we received a packet from the military at our home address. Joe brought the packet to Houston. I read the enclosed paperwork to Joey. The wording sounded right, but I wasn't comfortable with Joey signing anything until I had an attorney look the packet over. The paperwork had a deadline. By the time Joe got it to us in Houston, we only had a week to reply.

I decided to contact a lawyer familiar with military law. I called our family attorney back home. He gave me the name of a military attorney in Utica. Joe emailed this attorney, attaching a copy of the paperwork for his review. Two days later, he still hadn't replied. I decided to look online for an attorney in the Houston area who was familiar with military law.

I contacted Jack Zimmermann. I didn't realize he was one of the most highly recognized trial lawyers in the country nor did I realize his former position in the Marine Corp. He was so wonderful to me. He had me fax the documents to him for review. He called Joey's commander to be sure the paperwork was being processed properly. Then, he called me back and told me the documentation was fine for Joey to sign. I thanked him very much for his time and consideration. He told me he would keep Joey in his prayers.

After I hung up the phone, I received a phone call from the lawyer in Utica. He had called Joey's commander as well. He, too, said Joey would receive the discharges he deserved. I told Joey the news. He signed the forms and I sent them by certified mail from MD Anderson. Joey received his official discharge notification letter in April, which stated his discharge would be honorable and medical effective May 10, 2013.

Part of me was happy Joey got the discharge he deserved, but part of me was sad. This cancer had destroyed another one of Joey's dreams.

Joey Celebrates His Birthday

Joey was still in the hospital recovering from complications from chemotherapy when he celebrated his twenty-second birthday on March 11, 2013. Alicia, Joe, and Joey's best friend Michael flew down to Texas to celebrate his birthday. Joey loved having all of us there, especially Michael. He knew Michael had never flown before and he had traveled a long way to see him. Michael stayed for four days before returning home. Joey told me he had a wonderful birthday.

A week later his cousin, James, flew down to spend a few days with him. This became another special memory for Joey.

Discharge Day Arrives

On April 12th, Joey was strong enough to be discharged. I was the only one with Joey because Joe had to return home for a few days. The chronic pain doctors told me Joey would be discharged on a PCA of Fentanyl along with Methadone pills. He would not have a continuous rate of Fentanyl on his PCA but a set bolus every eight minutes. Fentanyl is a controlled substance, so his PCA would be monitored by a home health agency. Follow-up appointments were scheduled with his oncologist and pain doctor.

Since I would be the one taking care of Joey's weekly PICC dressing and cap changes, the hospital required me to attend a training session. The training taught me the proper sterile technique. After the training, I had a mandatory PICC bandage changing observation on Joey prior to his discharge.

At 4PM Joey and I returned to our room at the Rotary House. We found ourselves back in the hospital ER five hours later. To say we were agitated would be an understatement. I had attempted to hook Joey up to his TPN and the PICC cap wouldn't flush. At the training, I was told never to force flush a cap. If resistance was encountered the cap was probably blocked by a blood clot. The protocol was to call the Infusion Clinic or report to the ER (after normal business hours).

Joey's PICC had two caps, but one cap was being used by the PCA pump to deliver his pain medication. He had to have his TPN, therefore I had to bring him to the ER. I put him in a wheelchair and pushed him across the enclosed bridge to the adjoining hospital's ER.

We waited three hours for an infusion nurse. She injected the clot buster and the line opened in less than five minutes. Joey was hooked up to his TPN and we were cleared for discharge. By the time we got back to the hotel room, we were exhausted.

Leaving The Rotary House

I was getting stir crazy in a one bedroom, one bathroom living situation so we checked out of the Rotary House on April 20th. Cancer itself is stressful, but living in a hotel day in and day out just adds to the pressure. We needed some normalcy in this uprooted roller coaster of a life we were living. I decided to rent an affordable two bedroom, two bathroom apartment five minutes from the hospital. The apartment was located on the first floor of a gated complex and cost the same per day as our hotel room, including utilities.

It took half a day to move our belongings. We really liked the place because it had great bedding, plenty of towels, and brand new cookware. I made sure the bedding was checked for bed bugs and all the mattresses were encased in sealed plastic covers. The apartment came with a washer, dryer, dishwasher, and microwave. No more washing dishes by hand or waiting for machines to open in the hotel laundry room. Best part, I could make Joey some of his favorite meals.

A Sister's Love

Alicia was eighteen months old when Joey was born. As they grew, many people thought they were twins because of their age proximity and height. Alicia always said, "I can't remember a time in my life when Joey hasn't been with me."

When Joey left for boot camp, Alicia cried. She loved her little brother and had never been far away from him. She wrote him letters all the time and kept track of his unit on the Fort Jackson web site. She was so happy to hear his voice when he called her. You can't imagine how thrilled she was to have him home for her birthday and wedding. Everyone told us the timing of his Army graduation was amazing. Looking back, it was a precious gift from God.

Nothing could prepare Alicia for the night her little brother was diagnosed with cancer. Her world was shattered. Since Joey's diagnosis, I worried about her. I knew, at times, she felt like the forgotten child. It was difficult for me to be so far away when I knew she needed me too.

Alicia helped Joey in so many ways. She was a wonderful sister. Joey's face would light up every time she came to see him. He cherished every moment he had with her, especially now that he was sick. He told me often how much he loved and missed her. He would say, "She is my beautiful, brown-eyed Sis."

I could tell Alicia felt the same way. Her face would shine when she saw Joey. I couldn't imagine how she felt knowing she may lose her little brother and best friend. One thing I knew for certain – if a sister's love could cure cancer, Joey would have been cured long ago.

6

Casualty of War

"I cannot conceive of a greater loss than the loss of one's self-respect." — ***Mahatma Gandhi***

Right after Joey's discharge, on April 12th, things seemed to be going well. Then, I began to notice a change in Joey's behavior. He started to go into the bathroom more frequently and for longer periods of time. I could tell trouble was brewing and suspected an issue with his pain medication.

I checked his PCA and noticed the pump readings were slightly off. Then, one night before bed, Joey started to act strange when he came out of the bathroom. He sat on the edge of the bed and struggled to stay awake. When I asked him what he had done, he smiled at me. I checked the PCA settings and discovered his bolus setting had been significantly increased. I was horrified...was he going to stop breathing?

I called the pharmacist at the home health care agency. He had me check Joey's respiratory rate. His rate was low but still within normal limits. The pharmacist instructed me and I changed the bolus dosage back and locked out the pump. Now, Joey wouldn't be able to alter the settings.

Apparently, Joey had been slowly increasing his bolus. Finally, he overshot his threshold causing him to display symptoms. The pharmacist told me most people would have stopped breathing at the level Joey had reached, but over time, Joey's body had developed a tolerance to the drug. To Joey, it was no big deal. He just wanted freedom from the pain and stress he was under day in and day out.

Alicia happened to be visiting and we spoke with him. He apologized and promised he wouldn't do it again. My heart was pounding in my chest and my anxiety was out of control. What if he had overdosed? How would I live with myself?

Alicia told me Joey was a grown man and he was responsible for his own actions, not me. She reassured me I was a good mom and I was doing a great job. I appreciated her pep talk, but I was still scared. I called Joe at home and told him what Joey had done. He was very upset but relieved that Alicia was with me. He knew she would help me keep an eye on him.

Five days later, Joe flew back to Texas and Alicia returned home. Joe had a firm talk with Joey. He told Joey how much he loved him and worried about him. He said, "I understand why you want to increase your medication, but this behavior is simply not acceptable." Reassuring his Father, Joey told him he understood and he would stop.

Two days later, Joey was lingering in the bathroom for an extended period of time. I knocked on the door and asked him if he was okay. He told me his stomach was off. When he exited the bathroom, he had glassy eyes. I confronted him and he admitted to finding a way around the pump's lock out. Fearing he would overdose, I disconnected the PCA. I told Joey we couldn't trust him to do the right thing so we were going to do it for him. I picked up the phone and called his pain doctor.

The Reckoning

As I was telling the pain doctor the history of Joey's recent Fentanyl abuse, Joey fell to pieces in the adjoining room. Joe went to him and put his arms around him. He told him how much we loved him.

At that moment, all the pent up emotions Joey had been carrying inside of him for months came pouring out. He told us how he was ruining our time together, his sister's marriage, and using up all of our life savings. He told us his quality of life was gone. Through tears, he told us how angry he was and how he resented having to live his life like this. How none of his hopes and dreams would be achieved or even attempted. He wanted to get away from it all, to be happy again, and the higher dose of Fentanyl helped him do this. If he could get drunk, he would do that instead. But he couldn't drink with the opiates he was taking.

Soon, all three of us were crying and hugging one another. Joey was finally coming to terms with the nightmare he was living. I can still remember how frightened I felt for him, how helpless, and how powerless. I begged God to look down on Joey with mercy.

Joey told us he was embarrassed by what he had become, calling himself a junky. We told him the Fentanyl was given to him as a result of the circumstances he was in, not because he went out seeking it. Joe told him that many cancer patients become addicted to these drugs because these drugs trigger addiction. I told him he needed to address the underlying reasons behind his behavior and the first step was to get him to the hospital. Joey agreed. He composed himself and the three of us went to the ER.

Joey had become close to Dr. Regina while in the hospital with his BEP complications. She met us in the ER to avoid any embarrassment for Joey. She was glad to be there to support him. She led the three of us into a conference room. There, she told Joey not to be embarrassed about his behavior and stressed the importance of expressing his feelings. She asked him if he ever had thoughts of suicide. He said, "No, I have never thought of doing anything like that." She asked us to leave the room so she could speak to Joey in private. She had a brief conversation with him and then motioned for us to return. Giving each of us a hug, she told Joey she would check on him in the morning.

Six hours later, the ER doctor admitted Joey for pain management. He was placed on a hospital PCA and his other medications were continued as assigned. The hospital was ninety-nine percent full so we ended up spending the night in the ER. Joe and I tried to sleep in the same recliner with little success.

Around 9AM, Dr. Wells came to see us. He apologized for the lack of hospital beds and told us he would get Joey into a hospital room as soon as one became available.

Treating the Whole Person

After Dr. Wells left, the psychiatrist Joey had met the first week we arrived came to see him. We were happy to see her. Joey's pent up stress and anxiety indicated he needed to have a discussion with her.

She spoke to Joey alone, then she called us into the room. She asked us a series of simple questions regarding Joey's mood, sleep, and appetite. Then she told us she was going to increase his antidepressant and add a new medication to help with his sleep and appetite. She told us she wanted to see Joey in her office in two weeks, unless he wished to see her sooner. We were relieved to know Joey was getting the help he needed.

A Bed at Last

We had been in the ER for seventeen hours when a bed became available. As soon as we entered the hospital room, Joe opened the fold out bed and I flattened the sleeper chair. I was so exhausted I felt nauseous. We settled in for some needed rest.

Early the next morning, the chronic pain team came to visit. The pain doctors had a frank conversation with Joey about his Fentanyl abuse. Joey told them he had started to increase his Fentanyl shortly after his discharge. He was told he would never be discharged on a home PCA again. Instead, his Methadone pills would be increased to act as a better baseline and he would be given a Fentanyl lollipop every four hours for break-through pain. This new regimen would be assessed for the next twenty-four to forty-eight hours. If they felt his pain was well managed, he would be discharged.

We knew that Joey was in physical and emotional pain and we were worried about keeping him pain free should his disease progress. We prayed we would be able to help with whatever future needs he may have.

The Third Day Was a Charm

By April 23rd, the third day in the hospital, Joey's pain was under control. The pain doctors felt he was ready for discharge. Joey was relieved because he was sick of being in the hospital. He was discharged on Methadone, Gabapentin, and Fentanyl lollipops.

We were leery of his honesty, so we kept the Fentanyl locked in the car and brought just enough into the apartment to last for a day.

On An Even Keel

To our relief, Joey did great on the new regimen. So, I began to concentrate on Joey's G-tube. The surrounding tissue needed to heal for him to pursue further treatment. Joey would clean the area daily and apply a layer of Desitin to help the irritation. I would administer his daily IV antibiotics.

On April 24th, we met with Dr. Zinner in the targeted therapy clinic. Due to BEP and PCA complications, Joey hadn't received chemo for eight weeks. Dr. Zinner reviewed Joey's medical history and blood results with us. Then, he told Joey he needed to get another PETCT to act as a baseline before starting any treatment.

He recommended two targeted drugs – Xalkori (Crizotinib) and Votrient (Pazopanib). He told us Votrient was known as an angiogenic inhibitor. Simply put, this drug stops the development of new blood vessels that feed tumors; thereby, shrinking or killing the tumors. The Xalkori would block a chemical signal that tumor cells release when their blood supply is under attack. All tumors make blood vessels to supply them with nutrients, so he felt both drugs would be good to try on Joey's tumor.

He said, "Both drugs are in pill form so Joey can take them as an outpatient and very little side effects have been noted when these drugs are used at reduced doses. I will petition the insurance company for approval of both drugs."

He also wanted Joey's tumor to be analyzed at the molecular level, so he sent some tumor samples to Foundation Medicine. We would get the results in six to eight weeks.

I asked him about a clinical study I had read where a woman with an unusual form of DSRCT had her CA-125 levels monitored. In her situation, the CA-125 levels would increase when her tumor was not responding to chemo and decreased when the tumor was responding. I asked if we could test Joey's CA-125 levels. He said, "I will be glad to do it. However, several factors can affect CA-125 levels in the body." Dr. Zinner scheduled Joey's PETCT for the next morning.

The Scan

Joey got his scan done at 10AM the following day. That afternoon, we returned to the targeted therapy clinic to review the results. We were on pins and needles as we waited for Dr. Zinner. He entered the room, sat down at the computer, and opened up Joey's PETCT file. Joey pulled his wheelchair up to see the screen and I sat beside him.

Dr. Zinner went over each part of the scan with us starting at Joey's head and working down through his abdomen. There was good news and bad news. The good news was two areas in Joey's lower lungs were clear when they had previously shown signs of possible metastasis. The bad news was the cancer had grown twice in size on the lower right side of his abdomen and there were three lymph nodes in his chest showing signs of metastasis. Bottom line, during his chemo hiatus, the cancer had grown back in the previously shrunken areas and had spread further into the abdomen.

Dr. Zinner told us not to worry about the lymph nodes in the chest. He told Joey to stay positive as the cancer spread, but not as aggressively as it could have after eight weeks without treatment. He told me Joey's CA-125 levels were greatly elevated. If Joey's results were similar to those I had read about, then his tumor growth was starting to accelerate. Dr. Zinner told Joey he wanted to start him on the targeted chemo as soon as possible.

Christus Stehlin Foundation & Caris Life Sciences

Dr. Zinner excused himself and a resident oncologist came in to discuss Joey's case. I told him we had sent fresh tumor samples from the blockage surgery, in January, to a research lab in Texas called the Christus Stehlin Foundation. The lab focuses on DSRCT and tries to grow patient's tumor samples on mice. If the growing process is successful, the tumor cells are used to test new treatments. Since Pittsburgh pathologists suspected DSRCT, we wanted the lab to have some of Joey's tumor.

The resident suggested I call the lab to see if the tumor had grown and if they had tested the cells. He told us about another company called Caris Life Sciences. This company attempts to grow the tumor on mice as well. The grown tumor cells are then treated with existing chemo drugs to discover which chemotherapy drugs work the best against it. This process takes three to six months. Growing the tissue takes the longest amount of time. The drug testing itself takes two to four weeks. In some cases, the tumor is never successfully grown so the cells cannot be tested. I thanked him for the tip. I decided to call Christus Stehlin and investigate Caris.

As soon as I arrived back at the apartment, I called the Christus Stehlin Foundation. I spoke to Doug Coil, whom Joe had dealt with in January when we had sent samples of Joey's tumor. He told me he would talk to the researchers to see if Joey's tumor had grown. If Joey's tumor had grown, their lab would be willing to share his live tissue with Caris.

Next, I investigated Caris Life Sciences. After reading about their research, I decided to give them a call. The research representative I spoke with told me their researchers needed fresh tumor samples. I knew obtaining a fresh sample from Joey wasn't possible. So, I told her about the Christus Stehlin Foundation and the fresh sample they had from Joey's surgery in January. She told me they could have some of the tissue sent to them if it was successfully growing, or the entire mouse could be sent to them. Hearing this gave me some hope for Joey' s situation. She e-mailed the necessary consent forms.

As I was looking the forms over, Doug called back. He told me Joey's tumor wasn't growing, but the researchers were going to continue to watch the mice for another few months. He said some tumors take longer than others to grow. Should Joey's tumor grow he would notify me.

I was hoping we could find the right chemo medications to kill Joey's cancer by using these two companies. Now, this was no longer an option for us. Joey was running out of time. I had to hope the targeted drugs would be the answer to our prayers.

PAP

Another week passed by without treatment. We were anxious to get some form of chemo started. I couldn't stand the thought of the cancer spreading in Joey's abdomen as the clock ticked away. I checked our mailbox and there was a letter from the insurance company. Great news – Votrient was approved for one year. I was so excited that I sent Dr. Zinner an email. He was very happy for Joey. He would contact Dr. Wells so Joey's treatment could begin.

Two days later, we had our weekly blood work and clinic visit with Dr. Wells. He told us he was going to start Joey on the lowest possible dose of Votrient, 200mg, due to his elevated liver function and bilirubin.

We picked up the prescription at the pharmacy and Joey began treatment on May 3, 2013. Of course, we didn't know how Joey would react so we were nervous. Thankfully, he had no negative side effects. To the surprise of both Dr. Wells and Dr. Zinner, Joey's elevated bilirubin and liver functions started to decrease. Dr. Wells told us he wouldn't do another PETCT on Joey until he had been on the targeted chemo for six to eight weeks. Unless, he suspected the cancer wasn't responding.

After two weeks on Votrient, I received another letter from the insurance company. The Xalkori was denied. I contacted Dr. Zinner. He wrote an appeal letter. Again, coverage was denied.

Dr. Zinner told me not to be discouraged. He contacted PAP (Patient Assistant Program). PAP required Joey to sign some paperwork and provide them with a copy of his most recent income tax. PAP sent the paper work to the drug company making the chemo pill. If approved, the drug manufacturer would pay for Joey's medication.

Another week passed and Joey continued to do well on the Votrient. His bilirubin and liver functions spiraled downward towards normal levels. Dr. Wells was considering increasing his dose to 400mg but he didn't want to do this if the Xalkori was going to be added. He decided to wait.

The next day, PAP called. Joey was approved. He would receive Xalkori for one year at a daily dose of 250mg. The medication would be shipped monthly to him by a specialty pharmacy. I was so happy to share the news with Joey and his oncologists.

It Could Be So Many Things

Joey started the Xalkori on May 25th. He had been doing so well on the Votrient, we were hesitant to add the additional drug. The next morning Joey woke up with nausea that lasted until noon. I gave him Zofran and the nausea subsided. I decided it would prudent to give Joey Zofran prior to his taking the Xalkori. No sense having nausea if it could be avoided.

That evening, Joey said he was feeling some pressure in his G-tube area. I told him one of the side effects of Xalkori was constipation. I recommended he increase his fluid intake and stay on a semi-solid diet for a day or two.

Just before bed, he got himself a glass of Kool-Aid. As soon as he drank some, the liquid leaked out from around the G-tube. He showed me the wet gauze padding. I removed the gauze to take a look at the area. The Kool-Aid was dripping from his skin underneath the tube. I cleaned the area with warm water, applied Desitin ointment, and covered the site with another gauze pad. Joey kept an eye on the site for further leakage. We decided to call the doctor in the morning. I didn't sleep a wink that night because I was terrified Joey was developing another blockage. I prayed this wasn't the case.

The next morning, I called the surgeon's office. The assistant said she wanted to see Joey in the clinic in two days. If his G-tube began to leak heavily or he experienced any increased abdominal pressure, he would have to report to the ER. My mind was spinning with worry because his symptom could be the result of so many things. He could be constipated from the chemo or pain medications, a blockage could be forming from the cancer, or the balloon in his G-tube could be deflating.

Over the next two days, I tried my best to hide my anxiety as I waited for our scheduled visit. Needless to say, Joey was more anxious than me.

The Clinic Visit

At the clinic, Dr. Hayes-Jordan asked Joey a series of questions. Then, she sent him for an abdominal x-ray. After the x-ray was taken, we returned to the clinic to hear the results. She said, "There is no apparent blockage." I could feel the stress pour off me. She felt Joey was suffering from constipation and prescribed Miralax.

She was also concerned the Votrient could be causing the G-site to leak. Votrient attacks areas of the body that are healing. She had actually seen newly healed incisions reopen during its use. To be safe, she prescribed an antibiotic. We left the clinic delighted that Joey didn't have a blockage, but concerned that his G-tube site may be reacting to the Votrient.

Chemo Reaction or Impending Blockage

Joe flew home on June 2nd and Joey started to have severe abdominal pain and increased nausea right after he left. He spent most of the day lying on the couch holding his stomach. He told me he hated how he felt and he wondered if living through this cancer was going to be worth it. He said, "I don't know if I will be able to live with short gut syndrome, nightly TPN, and daily chemo pills. Not to mention the twenty-five pills a day I am taking to manage my pain and bilirubin." I told him I understood where he was coming from, but his quality of life could improve once the cancer was under control. Over the past few months I could see the fight slowly draining from him. I could tell he was thinking of going home and closing his eyes.

As the hours passed, Joey's pain increased. By late evening, he was in a fetal position on the couch failing to find any relief. He told me the pain was constant and it stretched across his abdomen just under his belly button. I knew he couldn't continue like this. I emailed Dr. Zinner and Dr. Wells. Dr. Zinner responded right away. He felt the symptoms could be toxicity from the Crizotininb. He told me he would be returning to the clinic in two days. Meanwhile, he would check into Joey's symptoms with a fellow doctor he knew who was running a Crizotinib trial. If Joey needed immediate care, he suggested we contact Dr. Wells. I checked my email again and Dr. Wells had responded. He told me he was in Chicago. He told me to discontinue the Crizotinib and to bring Joey to the clinic in the morning to see his on-call doctor.

We slept very little that night, Joey due to pain and me due to worry. We drove to the clinic at 8AM. Alicia called while we were on route. She told me her plane had landed at Bush International and she needed an address for the cab driver. I told the clinic address and informed her of Joey's situation. Upon arrival at the clinic, Joey was taken in for blood work. After his blood was drawn, we returned to the waiting area. Moments later, Alicia arrived with her suitcase in tow. Joey's eyes lit up when he saw her. She ran over and gave him a big hug. He had the first smile I had seen on his face since the pain had begun.

The on-call oncologist called us in and introduced himself. He asked Joey a series of questions, examined his abdomen, and told him his blood work came back normal. He said, "Crizotinib is known to cause constipation, diarrhea, nausea, and vomiting." But he wasn't certain it would cause the type of abdominal pain Joey was experiencing. He told us he had spoken with Dr. Wells prior to calling Joey into the exam room. Dr. Wells was worried about a possible intestinal blockage.

Joey said, "The pain doesn't feel like the pain I had with my previous blockage." The oncologist decided to stop the Crizotinib. He advised me to give Joey a liter of IV fluid when we returned to the apartment. He told Joey to keep track of his bowel movements and to follow-up with Dr. Wells at the clinic when he returned.

Alicia, Joey, and I left the clinic and returned to the apartment. I gave Joey his liter of fluid over two hours. His pain remained stable for the rest of the day but my concerns increased. Joey still hadn't had a bowel movement. If he was getting a blockage what could be done? I was scared that the events currently happening were going to decide who would ultimately win this battle.

I prayed fervently. I asked the Lord to help my son at this crucial time. As my mind wandered, I remembered what my mother had told me long ago, "Trying times are times to try more faith." I knew I had faith but I was frightened. I couldn't imagine how Joey was feeling.

I knew we were both happy to have Alicia with us. I had spoken to Joe several times over the phone. He said, "I will fly there in a heartbeat if you guys need me." I knew he was more stressed than I was. It's always harder on someone when they are far away from the ones they love. Before bed, I gave Joey some stool softener hoping for an easy fix.

Suffering Due to Chronic Pain Services

The stool softener seemed to help Joey but his relief was short lived. As the evening progressed, Joey's abdominal pain intensified. He woke me and asked me to hook his G-tube to a drainage bag to help decompress his bowel. I hooked his tube up and nothing drained from his stomach into the bag. This terrified me.

He began to burp. Then, he quickly walked into the bathroom and I heard him vomiting. As I got him some Zofran, my stomach was in knots. Had our worst fears come true?

I called the outpatient floor at MD Anderson and spoke to a resident oncologist. He asked me a series of questions that I directed to Joey. He told me Joey could stay home until morning as long as the pain was tolerable and he didn't vomit again. Joey decided to sleep on the couch. Periodically, I would check on him. Most of the night he slept upright holding a pillow against his stomach.

At 7:30AM we reported to the clinic. Joey was in extreme pain and he was petrified of another blockage. I silently prayed a series of Hail Marys and Our Fathers as we waited. I asked the Lord to help Joey endure this cross he was baring. Several times, Alicia and I gave him a hug and told him how much we loved him.

The nurse led us to an exam room and the same on-call oncologist came in. He asked Joey a series of questions and examined him. He suspected an obstruction, so he ordered x-rays and blood work. He put Joey on IV fluids and gave him a bolus of Fentanyl. Joey was in so much pain that 100mcg of Fentanyl gave him little relief. He looked pathetic as he sat in the wheelchair with his head down holding his stomach. Alicia and I were on the brink of tears watching him.

I tried to console him by placing my arm gently around his shoulder. I held his hand and periodically kissed the top of his head. As a mother, I felt the need to ease his pain but I couldn't.

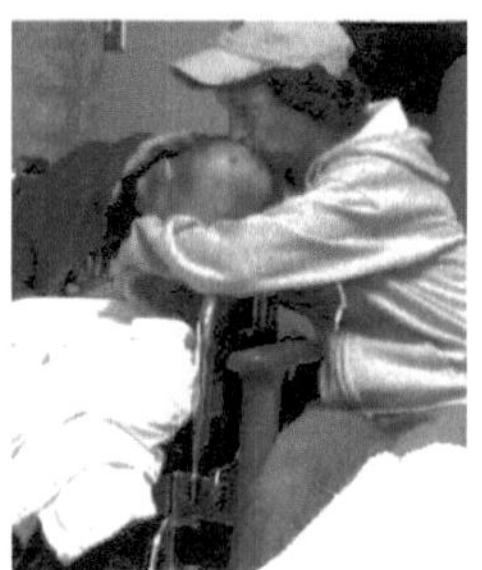

I try to comfort Joey

Before Joey had his x-rays he told the doctor it would be too painful for him to lay flat. The doctor was very compassionate. He ordered the radiographs to be taken in a standing position. The morning progressed slowly and Joey's pain hovered at a nine. To our frustration, the oncologist contacted chronic pain numerous times and they never came. Alicia and I were furious.

Around noon, Joey was admitted and assigned a bed on the pediatric oncology floor. We were hoping his pain would be addressed once we arrived there, but we were mistaken.

On the floor, I kept asking the nurses to flush the G-tube, but none took the time. I knew Joey's tube was blocked because nothing was draining into the drainage bag and he was complaining of pressure. Joe began to vomit into a nearby garbage can. I paged his nurse and asked for nausea medication. When she saw how sick he was, she quickly administered it. The nausea remained until his G-tube was flushed.

After flushing, tons of green liquid came pouring out. I couldn't prevent myself from saying, "If his tube had been flushed hours ago, he wouldn't have been suffering from intense nausea and pressure for so long." The nurse agreed. All of the day's events were annoying me.

The chronic pain PA finally showed up – twelve hours after Joey had arrived in the hospital! He told Joey he would give him Methadone by IV along with Fentanyl. The PCA of Fentanyl would be 30mcg every ten minutes with a nurse bolus every three hours. We knew this was not going to be enough. Joey's home PCA dose, when he was stable, was 50mcg every eight minutes. Why would a pain doctor start treatment on a patient who has lost their baseline at a dose lower than what he was receiving at home?

Joey sat in bed, bent over in pain, level nine, for another hour and fifteen minutes before the PCA was hooked up – so much for timely relief. I contacted Joe and told him what was going on. He was not happy. Joey suffered for the rest of the night despite several attempts to get pain service back to see him. He sat on the edge of the bed gripping his IV pole. Alicia and I could do nothing to help him, except repeatedly ask the nurses to page the pain doctors.

Alicia slept on the couch in Joey's room. I was going to sleep in the recliner, but Joey asked me to sit next to him in his hospital bed. I placed my arm around him so he could lay his head on my shoulder. I tried to stay awake but I found myself nodding off. When I came to, Joey was sitting on the side of the bed with his head down and eyes closed. Still gripping his IV pole. He said, "I'm so tired of the pain, Mama. I can't deal with it much longer." I told him I was sorry for all he was going through. He said, "I hate cancer." I replied, "I hate cancer, too. I wish I could make your pain go away, Sunshine." With tears on his cheeks, he said, "I love you very much, Mama." I gently hugged him, kissed his forehead, and said, "I love you too."

Alicia heard us talking and came over to hug Joey. She told him she loved him very much. He told her he loved her, too. He laid his head on her shoulder and she held him. As I watched the two of them, I had all I could do to keep myself together. I could see the deep love pouring out of them, along with their grief. How my heart ached. Why did Joey have to suffer this way?

I had planned on my children being together long after I was gone. Now, the thought of Joey being gone and Alicia becoming an only child was more than I could bear. Why was God doing this? I kept trying to understand why, but I just couldn't. As I looked at them, I flashed back to them playing in the yard as toddlers, dressing up for Halloween, and opening Christmas gifts. I felt overwhelming pain and immense sadness.

That morning, a team of oncologists came in. They told Joey they didn't know why he was in so much pain. The x-rays hadn't shown a blockage. However, they were concerned about internal bleeding. His hemoglobin had dropped over night from 8.7 to 6.2. He would be given two units of blood followed by a CT scan with contrast. For the time being, his chemo pills would be discontinued.

Joey had his nurse page chronic pain again and again. After seven hours, the same PA came to see him. He spoke with Joey for ten minutes, than he adjusted the PCA to 40mcg and added Tylenol every six hours. To us, this was a joke. Joey told the PA his concerns, yet nothing was done to address the level of pain he was in. His pain remained intense and persistent.

BEP Failure

At 9PM, I read a copy of the preliminary CT scan report. I was devastated. Joey had several newly infiltrated lymph nodes in his abdomen, a small abscess under his G-tube, narrowing of his intestine in some areas with dilatation in others, and portions of the peritoneal cancer was spreading. This meant the targeted chemo drugs were not working.

Alicia read the report and her eyes told me she understood the news. She left the room to call Brandon. I called Joe at home to share the news. He was heartbroken. He said, "I will be on the next available flight to Houston." I told him I was sorry he had to hear the news over the phone.

After hanging up, I decided to review the report again. This time, I noticed his CT scan had been compared to a CT scan done in March. I went to the nurses' station and requested to see the oncologist or surgeon on duty. The nurse paged the resident and she came to Joey's room. Joey was interested in his results, so I had her review the CT report with us. As she did, I pointed out the comparison date and told her Joey had a more recent PETCT done on April 25th. I asked if this CT scan could be compared to the April PETCT instead of the one in March. She said absolutely.

If I was thinking correctly, most of the current findings were not new – which meant the tumor hadn't grown and the targeted chemo had been working. I believed this to be the case because the April PETCT showed new lymph node involvement and tumor growth in the same areas reported on the current CT scan. The abdominal abscess and small intestine narrowing and dilatation would be new findings. The resident told me she would let me know what the radiologist found from the comparison.

Just Admit you're in Over Your Head

Joey had another rough night with less than two hours sleep. Despite several calls to chronic pain services, not one doctor came to see him. By morning, Joey had lost the edge and he had all he could do not to cry out from the pain and fatigue. I was on my way to see a patient advocate when Dr. Wells stopped by. I told him the problems we were having with chronic pain services. He was not pleased and told me he would look into the matter immediately.

At noon, the same chronic pain PA came to see Joey. I thought to myself, "Here they have a patient in extreme pain calling them all night and they wait until noon to see him. How does this make any sense?" He told Joey he didn't know what to do for him. According to him, Joey had maxed out their service's capabilities. Joey had been paging him for pain relief and suffering for two straight days. Why had he waited so long to tell Joey this?

He told Joey he was going to refer him to palliative pain services because they could deal with his high opiate tolerance more effectively. He told us he would fill out transfer orders. Two hours later, I checked on his transfer orders and they still hadn't been signed. It was miserable seeing Joey suffer hour after hour. He had only slept six hours in two days.

We learned an important lesson that day… ask for palliative pain services if you have a terminal patient who has developed a high tolerance to pain medications. Don't waste your time with chronic pain services.

Palliative Pain Care

Joey remained in pain until the palliative pain doctor came to see him that afternoon. She told him she would change his PCA from Fentanyl to Dilaudid so his brain receptors could be cleansed. Apparently, Fentanyl floods the receptors in the brain over time and this causes individuals to require higher and higher doses of the drug to alleviate their pain. She told him the Dilaudid should help reverse this process. She also assured him the dose of Dilaudid would be sufficient enough to end the prolonged suffering he had been in.

By the time his PCA was switched over, his Father had arrived at the hospital. He was relieved to find Joey's pain being properly addressed. Within hours, Joey's pain dropped to a six. Finally, his pain was heading in the right direction and he was able to get some sleep.

Early the next morning, the floor's oncologist told us Joey's blood work was great. He was, however, adding a third antibiotic to Joey's regimen because his G-tube was still discolored and oozing.

A wound care nurse stopped by and checked the site. She provided me with antibiotic powder, special drainage bandages, and skin barrier. After she left, Dr. Wells stopped by to tell us the radiologist had compared the recent CT scan to the CT portion of Joey's April PETCT. According to the comparison, the tumor had not grown in the past month and there were no additional lymph nodes involved. The only differences noted were the constricted and dilated intestinal areas and the abscess under the G-tube site.

This news was what I had suspected when I requested the comparison. In this case, the cancer had stabilized. Dr. Wells complimented me for noticing the CT comparison dates and asking for another comparison. He said, "It was good thinking on your part."

The oncology team would work on Joey's pain control followed by his bowel and abscess issues. If Joey came out of this on his feet, then Dr. Wells would discuss future chemo treatment. He said, "If a blockage is found, surgery would be too dangerous for you Joe. The Votrient you have been taking would cause bleeding and wound healing issues." This deeply troubled me.

Palliative Pain Doctor with Compassion

Joey's pain control improved after palliative care took over. He was able to sleep five straight hours after their first medication adjustment. The next morning, the palliative pain doctor came to speak to us. This time she introduced another palliative doctor from her team. He shook our hands and placed a chair next to Joey's bed. He sat in the chair and looked directly at Joey.

In a very soft, articulate voice he began to ask Joey questions. He asked Joey what he knew about the cancer he had, how he was holding up over the past year, who he relied on to get through times like this, if he was afraid of dying, what about dying scared him the most, and what his plans were if he was told chemo treatment couldn't be continued. We listened to Joey's responses.

Joey told the doctor what he knew about his cancer and how his past fifteen months had been. He told the doctor he relied on family and faith to get him through the tough times. He told him he was afraid of how his death would be if his bowels were to become blocked.

The doctor reassured him saying, "Palliative care will make sure your symptoms are well controlled throughout your treatment, now, and at the end of your life. You will have as little pain as possible." He also told Joey his death would be natural, no tubes or life support. He pointed out all of Joey's prior chemo attempts had caused him to suffer serious complications resulting in extensive hospital stays.

He cautioned Joey saying, "Your oncologist may offer future chemo, but these treatments may not be in your best interest since they could affect your quality of life." I knew the doctor wanted Joey to have quality of life, but I also knew Joey's current chemo had been holding his cancer at bay. I hated the thought of Joey stopping the medication if it was working.

He told Joey how he would manage his pain now and in the future. He wanted to treat all of Joey – his emotional and spiritual pain along with his physical pain. Even though the doctor was very compassionate, it was difficult to see him interact with Joey as he discussed a peaceful death and the remainder of quality time with friends and family.

Amazingly, Joey never showed any emotion throughout his conversation with the doctor. I, on the other hand, fought to keep my torrent of emotions under control.

Palliative Doc Reaches Out to the Family

Next, the doctor turned his attention to us. He focused his gaze directly upon me asking, "How is Mom doing with all of this?" I told him it was difficult seeing Joey go through this. My voice cracked mid-conversation and I began to cry. I said, "Joey has a lot of emotion inside of him I wish he would let out." I felt helpless and powerless.

He walked over to me and held my hand in both of his saying, "It's okay to share your feelings. You need to let your emotions out too." Then, he hugged me.

He turned to Alicia. He asked her how she was doing. By this time, she was sitting next to me with one arm around my shoulder. She told him it was difficult to see her brother suffer like this as her eyes filled with tears. She shook her head and gazed down at the floor. He touched the top of her hand saying, "I understand."

Then, he turned his attention to Joe. He asked, "How are you doing, Father?" Joe didn't say a word but his eyes were full of tears and his cheeks were flushed. Everyone could see his pain and that spoke louder than words. He walked over and offered Joe a hug. Joe said, "It hasn't been an easy road, Doc."

After a few moments, he walked back over to Joey and took hold of his hand saying, "You have a family that loves you very much and this is a very good thing. I will take good care of you Joseph. It is a pleasure to meet you and your family." Then he quietly left the room. We knew Joey would be in good hands.

I stared at Joey. I couldn't imagine him not being there for me to see and talk with. He motioned for me to come to him and he gave me a hug. I began to cry. He said, "Let me get my pain under control first, Mom, then I'll worry about dying."

G-tube Scare

By Joey's fifth day in the hospital, our anxiety level was starting to come down. His pain was at a five and he was sleeping again. The rest made him look so much better. The oncologist stopped in. He told Joey he could try to eat or drink a little something. Joey drank four ounces of orange juice and ate half a donut. The food seemed to stay down and Joey felt good. He even walked around the unit with us.

A short time later, his nurse came in and offered him his morning medications. He took one pill with a sip of orange juice and grabbed the nearby garbage can to vomit. The nurse returned with IV nausea medication – so much for eating and drinking.

Joey was very discouraged. He sat on the edge of the bed until he felt better. Then, he asked me for supplies to change the bandages around his G-tube. He wanted to keep his mind busy. This particular day, the area had a lot of yellow drainage. He used baby soap and a warm washcloth to clean the skin. Followed by a warm water rinse.

As he was drying the site, the skin around the tube began to leak. I placed two towels under the bottom of the tube to trap the liquid discharge, but the liquid was coming out too rapidly. Both towels were soaked. At first, the discharge was yellow, like the orange juice he had drank, but soon it changed to blood. I paged the nurse for help.

She paged the oncologist and the oncology team was in Joey's room before we knew it. The team said they would page the surgery team. I cleansed the area again. This time. I strategically taped two gauze pads around the tube in hopes the site wouldn't leak. After completing the bandage, Joey asked his nurse to flush his G-tube. The nurse injected a large syringe full of water into the tube and met with resistance when she attempted to draw it out. Something was wrong. She asked Joey to stand up. As soon as he did, the water exited the tube into the attached bag. This meant there was an obstruction somewhere. We noticed the site would leak when Joey sat up, not when he stood. This was information Joey would share with the surgery team when they arrived.

I hated to see Joey so nervous but who could blame him? I would be wondering what was going on in my intestine too if this were happening to me. Joey sat in his room waiting for over an hour for the surgery team to come. We decided to take him for a walk around the unit to distract him. When we returned, the surgery team still hadn't arrived. Joey decided to sleep.

As he slept, I sat on the bed next to him. He laid his head on my shoulder. I knew he was frightened and I was frightened for him. To our frustration, the surgery team never came that night. The next morning Joey was very disturbed with the surgery team. As he slept, I watched Sunday mass on my laptop.

Mid-morning there was a knock at the door. It was a clergy volunteer. The volunteer blessed and prayed over Joey. He said, "Jesus is with you in your many sufferings and he has not forgotten you in your time of need." Joey told him he knew he was not alone and God must have a reason for making him take this journey. Then, he received Communion.

After the volunteer left, Joey and I decided to pass time playing Battleship. We had a good time. I really enjoyed seeing him smile and hearing him laugh.

It's All about Perspective

Everyone seems to focus on the physical turmoil when someone is facing cancer. They forget about the mental turmoil. I realized this back when my father had cancer. He suffered from anxiety, especially at night. He told me he couldn't turn his thoughts off so he could rest. Instead, he would think about the time he had left, how his death would feel, and if there was life after death. Of course, extreme panic and fear would overcome him.

Lately, I was recognizing the same behaviors in Joey. He was scared of the future because he didn't know how much time he had left. He was scared of the present because he didn't know what was happening inside of him.

Back in January, I looked at Joey's G-tube as a safety valve. Now, for the first time, I saw the tube through his eyes. How upsetting it must be for a young man his age to look down and see this tube sticking out of his side. He had the tube for five months and it took me this long to see the tube from a different perspective.

I realized, as I attempted to see things from his viewpoint, why he would argue with me about changing his G-tube dressing twice a day. To me, the dressing change was simple and could be done in ten minutes. I would think, "What's the big deal?"

Now, I thought about it from Joey's perspective. To him, changing his G-tube bandage was a constant visual reminder he had a cancer growing inside of him that was methodically shutting down his intestines. To him, changing his dressing was a constant reminder his life wasn't normal anymore. I saw life in his protruding G-tube, while he saw a vivid reminder of impending blockage and death.

Thanks for Stopping By

The surgery team showed up forty-eight hours after they were initially paged. The past few days of waiting was mental torture for Joey. I wish these young inspiring doctors had made a phone call to the floor if they weren't coming. At least notify Joey they were aware of the situation and would be coming at a later date. I believe what they did was inconsiderate and uncaring. We all know that waiting is never easy, but put yourself in his shoes when the waiting involves news of a possible blockage that would end your treatment.

Two resident surgeons introduced themselves. They told Joey they felt his tube had moved up too far in his stomach and needed to be pushed back and stabilized. Without hesitation, one resident pushed the tube back down an inch into his side. His abrupt action caused intense pain and Joey made a horrid face. He never acknowledged Joey's discomfort.

Instead, he simply opened up a package of antiseptic and applied the cream around the site. Joey said the antiseptic was extremely irritating to his skin. Again, the resident never responded. The other resident applied a G-tube stabilizer and both of them left without further comment.

As soon as they left, Joey stood up and his G-tube began to leak all over the place...talk about major frustration. I ran out of the room to see if they were still on the floor. I found one standing by the nurses' station. I told her what was happening. She told me the tube would leak until the skin around the area had healed. I asked her how to protect the skin from the stomach acid that was being discharged. She was of little to no help. She told me to keep applying the gauze pads as I had been doing.

All three of us were upset over the residents' lack of concern and how they addressed the leakage. I thought to myself, "Thanks for stopping by, so sorry my son disturbed your day." I returned to Joey's room and cleaned the area with warm water. I gently patted it dry and applied absorbent gauze with skin barrier around the stabilizer.

Joe looked online and found the same G-tube Joey had. The diagram showed the balloon in the stomach against the stomach wall holding the tube in place. This meant the resident had pushed the G-tube in too far. Joe sent a text message to Beth asking her about the situation. She told him he was correct. Joe loosened the stabilizer and gently pulled on Joey's tube until he felt slight resistance. Then he tightened the stabilizer. Joey stood up and sat down and his tube never leaked.

Next, we looked online for ways to prevent the acidic discharge from touching Joey's skin. I found a few good ideas such as the application of Maalox. I called the wound nurse twenty-four hour hotline and one of the nurses told me they would stop by Joey's room. This made me feel better because these nurses knew how to properly care for skin. I guess we had to get more aggressive about helping Joey ourselves.

We Are Not Alone

One morning, I went to the Family Room to catch up on missed text messages and phone calls. I was just finishing up my conversation with my mother when I noticed a man slightly younger than myself sitting on the couch. He sat there a few minutes with his eyes closed and then got up and walked out. I ended my phone conversation and decided to head back to Joey's room.

As I opened the door to the hallway, I saw the man leaning against the wall with his head down. I told him the Family Room was available if he wanted some privacy. He thanked me. I could tell he was upset. I asked him if he was okay. He softly said, "No, my fifteen year old daughter is passing away." I lightly touched his shoulder saying, "I'm so sorry." He told me his daughter had been fighting a rare form of sarcoma for the past five years without any relief or remission. She was ten years old when she got hit in the knee with a soft ball and a bump appeared on her leg. The bump became very sore over a short period of time, so they had a doctor check it. Cancer was discovered in her bone.

After four years of bone surgeries, various chemo treatments, and radiation, the doctors told her she should go home and enjoy the time she had left with her family. She refused to quit and they were referred to MD Anderson. She was undergoing treatment here and the tumor had spread despite all of the oncologists' efforts. Now, the cancer was in her bones, brain, and lungs. A recent CT scan detected over a dozen small tumors in her brain. As tears streamed down his face, he told me how hard she had fought to live.

I shared Joey's story with him. We both understood how this roller coaster of life felt. Joe and Joey had been walking around the unit when they came upon us. Right away they knew something was wrong. I told them about the man's daughter. Joey gave the man a hug saying, "I'm deeply sorry." The man said, "Never forget your faith and remember the Lord is always with you." I felt the man needed some time with Joe since it would be one father leaning on another. So, I asked Joey to walk the unit with me.

Being part of a situation like this makes you reflect on your own. As Joey and I walked, he told me how he wished he were the teenage girl. He told me how difficult it was to be waiting until it was your turn...not knowing if it would be tomorrow, next week, or next month. The waiting alone caused him extreme anxiety. To him, the teenage girl was finally being set free. Free from the pain and suffering she had endured for so long. Her journey was coming to an end and she would finally be at peace. He said, "Soon, she will be in Heaven where she will be happy and healthy again. I am looking forward to that day even though it will be difficult on you, Dad, and Alicia. Palliative Care and Hospice will make sure I am comfortable. Hopefully, I won't know what's happening, but you will be the ones left to see it. I'm sorry my death will be like that for all of you."

He stopped walking, looked at me with watery eyes, and gave me a long, firm hug. I held him close saying, "I understood your feelings and I'm sorry." He said, "That's okay, Mom." I replied, "No, it's not okay, Joey, but I can't change it. You are my Sunshine. I love you very much and I'll miss you even more."

We made our way around the unit and back where Joe was waiting for us. He told us the girl's father had taken him in to see his daughter. He had introduced him to his wife and three children. Joe shared their sorrow with us – he told us the mother and older sister looked exhausted as they stood at the bedside. The daughter looked peaceful.

During his conversation with the girl's father, Joe told him how his ordeal with Joey had caused him to become angry with God. The girl's father told Joe he must never lose faith or be angry with the Lord. He said, "The Lord will be welcoming all of us one day – just as he will be welcoming my daughter soon and your son later on."

Joe's statement reminded me that I had purchased two brown scapulae when Joey got sick. Joey wore one. The other was kept in my purse. I decided to bring the second scapula to the young girl's hospital room. I knocked on the room door and a voice told me to come in.

As I entered the room, I could see the man sitting in a chair at the foot of his daughter's bed. A young boy, about five or six, was sitting in a chair next to him playing on a laptop. He never looked up. An older boy, around twelve, was looking at his laptop as he sat on a couch across the room. The man's daughter was lying in bed with a white blanket covering her up to her neck. Her long black hair fell softly around her face and she looked peaceful.

He told me his wife and daughter had gone to the Family Room. He stood up and introduced the two boys to me. They both nodded. I turned my attention to his daughter. I told him she was beautiful. He told me she was good unless the nurses changed her. Then he would leave the room because she would scream in pain. I could see the agony in his eyes.

I handed him the scapula and told him he could put it on his daughter if he wished, but he didn't have to. I told him it had been blessed. He thanked me. I told him we were next door if he, his wife, or family needed anything. As I was leaving, I saw him walk towards his daughter with the scapula in his hands.

That night, I blessed Joey with the Lourdes water and said my prayers from a different point of view. Now, I prayed for the Lord's will to be done and for Joey to have a peaceful death. I prayed for the teenage girl and her family. I asked the Lord to send an angel to escort their daughter to Heaven. Most of all, I asked the Lord to comfort her parents.

Love Thy Neighbor

The following morning, the hospital priest gave Joey the Anointing of the Sick. The priest asked Joey if there was anything he could do for him. Joey told him about the teenage girl and her family. He asked the priest if he could stop to see the family in case they wanted their daughter blessed. The priest told him he would be glad to visit the family for him.

Later that day, Joey and I stopped at the chapel to say a few prayers. On the way out of the chapel he filled out a prayer card for the young girl. Joey's actions throughout his illness reflected the Lord's words, "Love thy Neighbor". No matter how sick he was, Joey was always thinking of others.

Can Anyone Tell Us What's Up

Joey had been in the hospital for ten days now. At first, we feared another intestinal blockage. Day in and day out we worried the surgeon had missed something. But, she had taken three x-rays and a CT scan and had assured us there was no intestinal blockage, just a sluggish area of small bowel.

Dr. Wells told us he wanted to start the Votrient again. Joey's blood work was great and his pain was under control. We began to tell ourselves that we had been worrying about nothing. We were riding high when a resident oncologist stopped by. He said there was a change in treatment plans. The surgeon had decided to do a small bowel follow-through to be sure there was no hidden blockage.

Small Bowel Follow-Through

Early the next morning, Joey was taken down to radiology for the small bowel follow-through. Between scans, Joe and I were allowed to stay in the room with him. The technician clamped off his G-tube so the barium wouldn't drain out of Joey's stomach. He injected three ounces of contrast through the G-tube into the stomach and proceeded to take the initial images.

Thirty minutes later, the contrast was still sitting in Joey's stomach. It hadn't descended into the small intestine. Knowing the barium should have moved by now, I became concerned.

The technician placed a wedge behind Joey's back to tilt the stomach. Slowly, the contrast began to seep into the upper portion of the small intestine. Images would be taken forty-five minutes apart, and being nervous, Joey asked if he could walk around the hospital between takes. The technician told him he could. We walked all over the hospital between scans for the next five hours.

Five hours later, the contrast was less than half way through Joey's five feet of small intestine. The radiologist told Joey it normally took forty-five minutes for the contrast to travel through twenty-six feet of intestine. Clearly, Joey had a problem. She said she had seen adhesions and they could be causing a blockage. She sent Joey back to his hospital room. The remaining images would be completed at his bedside. Joey was scanned every forty-five minutes until 7PM.

We returned to the floor and Joey walked around the unit. He had been walking compulsively for the past three days. He told us it helped with his anxiety. We would walk laps around the unit and then take the elevator down to the first floor. There we would walk a loop outside and back inside the building and stop at the chapel for a prayer. Then we would walk through the cafeteria and take the elevator to the second or third floor.

Continuing on our journey, we would walk through the floors until we returned to the elevator and went up to the observation deck on the twenty-fourth floor. We would look out over Houston for a while and then return to the elevators and select another floor to walk. He was walking so often that my legs were starting to cramp. He detested being confined to his hospital room and he was anxious to get out.

During our walks, I left my cell phone number taped to his hospital room door. This way doctors and the radiology technician could call me when we needed to report back to his room.

That night, I blessed Joey with holy water and prayed the rosary. My faith was still intact but I was getting the distinct feeling Joey wasn't going to live much longer. I started changing my prayer focus. Instead of asking the Lord for a cure, like I had been praying for, I prayed for the Lord's will to be done. I asked Mary to give Joey strength and peace. Sadness, despair, and heartache consumed me as I prayed for strength to accept what I knew I couldn't change.

The Calling

Three days prior to Joey's small bowel follow-through, we were walking through the gift shop and Joey asked if he could buy a small prayer book. I purchased the book for him.

That night, Joe said his rosary and I prayed as Joey read the prayer book. I was amazed because Joey was never one to read, let alone a prayer book. Over the past few months he had seen his father and I pray for him and he had had several visits from priests and hospital clergy. He would receive communion when he could, and he often talked to me about God's will with his cancer, but this particular night he surprised us both. He told us he had a confession to make.

He said, "If I make it through this, I want to become a priest." He asked us how we would take that and if we wanted to laugh at him for thinking like this. We both told him we would be proud of him if he were to become a priest and we would never laugh at him for having the idea. He seemed pleased and thanked us.

Over the next few days, Joey spoke often of becoming a priest. He told us he wanted to have big weekly dinners at his parish so people could get to know one another. He said he wanted to be a priest so he could serve others. He visited the chapel several times a day and prayed. We couldn't believe the transformation we were seeing in him. I could tell something had happened to him, and for the first time in months, he seemed to be at peace with everything.

Joe was worried Joey was trying to make a deal with the Lord to spare his life – I didn't believe this to be so. I spoke to Joey and he clearly understood it might be too late for him to be a priest. He told me God would make the final decision. If he was able to overcome the cancer, he hoped the Lord would give him six to ten good years to serve him as a priest. If not, so be it.

Our Worse Fear Confirmed

Two days after the small bowel follow-through, the surgeon came in to see us. She told Joey the test had shown a blockage in his small intestine, about a foot from his stomach. The blockage was due to the cancer. The tumor had embedded itself into the muscle and surrounding tissue making it inoperable. He had a limited amount of bowel left negating a re-sectioning.

She recommended Joey keep his G-tube hooked up for decompression, continue his TPN for nutrition, and start chemotherapy to try to shrink the tumor. She told us Joey could eat small amounts of food but the food would pass directly into his G-tube and out of his body.

We had anticipated a blockage long before we heard the words to confirm it. Joey hadn't had a bowel movement in twelve days. Yet, the news was devastating to us. I found it hard to accept Joey would no longer be able to enjoy eating. He would be one hundred percent dependent on TPN. After the surgeon left, Joey told us he had a plan. He wanted Dr. Wells to do another PETCT and a repeat scan in a month to see if the Votrient was working. He knew his biomolecular results from Foundations Medicine should be reported to Dr. Zinner in a few weeks. Hopefully the results would give Dr. Zinner a specific chemo treatment to try. God Bless Joey, he still wanted to fight.

The Crow and the Stones

One of Joey's nurses was from India and she had a very strong faith in the Lord. She walked in his hospital room one morning and asked him how his small bowel follow-through went. Joey told her the news about the inoperable blockage. She smiled at him and told him never to lose faith. She asked him if he knew the story of the crow and the stones. He told her he did not. She proceeded to tell him the story.

There was a crow and he was very thirsty. He found a jar with a little water in the bottom but his beak was too short to reach the water. So, the crow picked up one pebble at a time and dropped it into the jar until the water was reachable by his beak. We all laughed. She told Joey that the pebbles indicated faith and he needed to keep working on his faith. Joey smiled at her and said, "The Lord's will be done."

Exiting in a Hurry Doesn't Pay

Joey was still walking endlessly about the hospital. I knew he was scared. How could anyone experience this reality without trepidation and fear?

The doctors were having problems balancing Joey's pain off the PCA. They were trying to transition him from IV medications to oral, and Joey was having difficulty with absorption as a result of the G-tube and intestinal blockage. The palliative pain doctors were trying to keep Joey in the hospital so they could transition him, but he was pushing for discharge. Joey was becoming increasingly anxious, acting like a caged bird. We thought he should give the transition a few more days, but he refused to listen. The doctors decided to give him a chance and discharge him on liquid Methadone every eight hours and liquid Dilaudid every three to four hours.

As soon as we arrived at the apartment, Joey started to have issues with pain control. He had to clamp the G-tube so he could retain the liquid medication in his stomach. He drank his Methadone and fifteen minutes later he unclamped the tube. As soon as he did, a portion of the medication would go directly into the attached drainage bag. The same happened with the Dilaudid.

We tried to clamp his G-tube for a longer period of time, but this resulted in vomiting. Joey wasn't receiving a full dose of medication. Therefore, he was slowly losing control of his pain. The on-call pain doctor suggested giving him his pain meds every two hours. We tried, but still most of the medication was being lost.

By midnight, just eight hours after his discharge, we had to return to the hospital. The on-call pain doctor had already notified the ER doctor so Joey was placed on a PCA of continuous IV Dilaudid. At 6AM, Joey was readmitted to the pediatric oncology floor.

7

Time to Decide

"Every tomorrow has two handles. We can take hold of it by the handle of anxiety, or by the handle of faith." — **Author Unknown**

The following days were challenging for Joey. The palliative pain team continued to make adjustments to his medications in a valiant effort to get him out of the hospital and off the PCA. They added pills into the regimen in place of liquids, but Joey was still asking for a bolus every three hours. They changed his medications back to liquid and he started to vomit them up.

They discussed pain blocks and a pain pump with chronic pain services. Given his current circumstances, the pain pump was decided against because it would require a surgical procedure and the likelihood of subsequent complications. A pain block was considered. However his white blood cell count was elevated and there was a fear of infection. Chronic pain decided against the block because they didn't want any bacteria traveling to the brain via the hole in the spine made by the injection.

The palliative doctor was worried because Joey was on 90mg of Methadone every eight hours and he was still asking for an 8mg bolus of Dilaudid every three hours. Nothing he did seemed to reduce the number of boluses.

Joey told the doctor he felt the Methadone pills weren't being absorbed. The doctor said some absorption was taking place because his heart's QT wave was reacting to the medication. After careful discussion, the doctor decided to try Methadone suppositories. Joey was not keen on the idea, but the pain doctor told him eighty-five percent of the medication is absorbed through the rectum when given in suppository form. So, Joey agreed to try them.

Dr. Wells had a long discussion with Joey about his future chemo treatment with Votrient. He said Joey's CT scan had shown stabilization of the tumor, but he also developed a blockage, so the tumor may have grown despite the evidence on the scan. Since the blockage was impeding Joey's absorption of medication by oral route, he thought IV medications would be of better use. He suggested two outpatient IV chemo drugs: Irinotecan and Temozolomide. Uncertain of how Joey would respond to these drugs, he suggested Joey sign an outpatient do not resuscitate (DNR) order.

The thought of losing Joey from his next chemo treatment made me sick to my stomach. I had been trying to stay positive for so long. I found myself questioning my faith and wondering if God had really been listening to our prayers. Immediately, in my heart, I knew the Lord had been listening. I was just bitter. I knew God was beside us all along. How else could Joey have made it this far? How else could he have endured his many sufferings?

After Dr. Wells left, a caseworker came in with the DNR form for Joey to sign. The hospital had a notary witness the signing and sign the form as well. After the caseworker and notary left the room, we spoke with Joey about his current situation. Joey decided it was time to return home in the event something went wrong with his chemo. He knew the drugs Dr. Wells had suggested could be done back home or in Pittsburgh. Joe and I agreed.

The next morning, we told Dr. Wells Joey's wish to return home for his remaining treatments. He thought this was a prudent decision given Joey's condition.

Joey told me he would like Dr. Bartlett to check his most recent CT scan for a second opinion regarding his inoperable blockage. If this were the case, I told him we should fly back to Pittsburgh first for a consultation there. He agreed. I promised Joey I wouldn't let him suffer with pain should he be facing an end-of-life situation. I decided to contact Dr. Maurer. Being a palliative pain doctor I knew he would be a good fit for Joey's current situation.

I called Dr. Maurer and he told me he would be glad to take care of Joey as his palliative pain doctor. In this capacity, he could work with him should he decide to return home on Hospice.

He spoke to his oncology department head and he was told Joey could come to Children's Hospital in Pittsburgh to become a patient of his. He would assess Joey for pain and for future chemo. Joey decided it was time to return to Pittsburgh.

Joey's Best Friends Come to Texas

Joey's best friend, Kyle, and his fiancée, Rachel, came to Texas to visit Joey the week before we flew back to Pittsburgh. Kyle and Rachel knew Joey was going through a difficult time and they wanted to show their support. Joey gave them both a hug. He was so happy to see them. Kyle asked him to be a groomsmen in his upcoming wedding. Joey said, "I hope I'm well enough to be there." At the time, the wedding was four weeks away.

Kyle, Rachel, and Joey had known each other since fifth grade. I had a good time watching the three of them laughing and sharing fond memories with one another. I flashed back to the times they were all hanging out together in my living room playing video games. I remembered yelling at Kyle and Joey for wrestling in the house. I was afraid they would break something or get hurt. Now, Joey looked so tiny and frail beside Kyle. A shell of the young man he once was. Noticing this overwhelmed me with sadness. I couldn't seem to make sense of the way things had turned out for him. I never imagined I would be wondering if Joey would live long enough to be part of his best friend's wedding.

I knew it was wrong, but jealousy overcame me. Jealous that Joey's friends would be able to have a life ahead of them, a future to look forward to and celebrate. I felt resentment because my son was having his future and quality of life slowly and painstakingly stripped away from him. I knew I shouldn't feel this way, but I couldn't help myself. I just felt my son had been dealt an unfair hand, a hand he didn't deserve.

Then I found myself looking around the cancer center asking myself, "Who deserves this?" One glance told me many others had been dealt the same hand as my son. Everywhere I looked, I saw people of all ages struggling with cancer. Each of them had their own story but all were facing the same fears. We weren't alone in the fight. Many parents were facing what I was facing and many patients were facing what Joey was facing. I closed my eyes and said a prayer for all of us because I knew none of us could get through this without God. We all needed help from a higher power.

During the visit, Joey asked Kyle to be one of his pallbearers. Kyle accepted with tears in his eyes. It was difficult for Kyle to hear Joey talk about his death. Kyle and Rachel told him his spot in the wedding party wouldn't be replaced because they would want him with them in spirit. Kyle told Joey he would always think of him as his brother. Joey thanked Kyle and Rachel. He told them both to let him know if they wanted to keep anything in particular of his to remember him by. He said the same to his sister. Alicia told him she wanted his favorite childhood stuffed animal. He said, "Baby Bunny is yours." He asked me if I wanted anything in particular. I told him everything he owned was sentimental to me so I would keep those items he didn't give away.

Kyle and Rachel stayed for two days and had a difficult time saying goodbye. Kyle told Joey to stay strong and he and Rachel would come to Pittsburgh to visit. As I gave Kyle a hug goodbye, he started to cry. I think Kyle finally realized the battle Joey had been fighting, and the harsh reality he was facing.

Making Plans for Home

On June 25th, Dr. Wells told me to go with Joey to the Imaging Library and the Medical Records Office to have all Joey's records sent to the doctors in Pittsburgh. He also told me to get a copy of Joey's imaging to take with me. I gave Dr. Wells the phone number to Dr. Maurer so they could talk about Joey's case.

Dr. Maurer called. He told me he had set up a consultation for Joey on July 3, 2013. He would assess Joey for pain and for possible future chemo treatment during the visit. If he felt Joey wasn't strong enough for chemo, he would place him in palliative care and send him home.

We decided to fly home with the same aviation company that flew us to Texas back in January. This time, I needed a nurse on board the plane to administer pain medication during and after the flight. Thankfully, we had come to know many nurses in Pittsburgh. I sent a text message to three of them explaining Joey's situation. Linda, a nurse Joey had on 6 PAV, responded. She told me she would love to fly down to Texas and make the return trip with us. We were so grateful she was willing to come.

Next, I had to coordinate Joey's TPN, medications, and the closing of our rental apartment in Houston. I contacted our corporate housing representative and submitted a letter to vacate the apartment on July 3rd. I called the specialty pharmacy and changed Joey's medication delivery date, and I contacted our home supply company and told them the situation and discussed TPN for the trip.

We planned on being discharged from MD Anderson by 9AM on July 3rd. Joey would get a bolus for his pain just before we left the floor. We would drive to Hobby Airport and leave our rent-a-car there. We would board the jet and Linda would be waiting inside for Joey. The flight back to Pittsburgh would take approximately two hours. Linda would give Joey a pain bolus as prescribed. In Pittsburgh, we would take a rental car to the Children's Hospital of Pittsburgh for Joey's 3PM consultation with Dr. Maurer.

Calm before the Storm

On June 27th, Joey woke up early complaining of abdominal pain and chills. He expressed concern about pressure and soreness around the G-tube to Dr Wells. Dr. Wells contacted the surgeon. The surgeon's assistant felt the area was agitated by the tube rubbing on the skin, despite the use of the stabilizer. She ordered an ultrasound for the following morning.

The next morning, Alicia decided to go to ultrasound with Joey so I could relax in the room and take a break. I was eating my breakfast when I received a text from Alicia. The text said, "Come to the third floor Imaging Center right away something is very wrong with Joey's G-tube." I ran down the hall and took the elevator to the Imaging Center.

As soon as I entered the room, I found Joey cupping his G-tube as greenish-yellow liquid spewed all over his stomach. As I got closer, I could see a round bronze colored object protruding from his skin. I could see pain and panic on Joey's face as Alicia stood next to him crying. The object was the balloon that held the G-tube in his stomach. It had pushed its way out of his abdomen during the ultrasound. The ultrasound technician just stood there staring at the sight. I asked her to call the ninth floor and tell the nurse a doctor or surgeon was needed in ultrasound right away. I took out my cell phone and told Alicia to stay with Joey as I went into the adjacent hallway to call Dr. Regina. I received a return call in less than two minutes. I told the nurse what was happening and she told me she would page Dr. Regina.

Meanwhile, Joey was asking for a bolus to reduce his pain. I called the ninth floor and asked if his nurse could bring him a pain bolus. Five more minutes passed, which felt like an eternity, and still no doctor or nurse in sight. I called Beth. She answered on the second ring. I told her what was happening. She told me not to panic because this particular situation looked scarier than it actually was. She told me to deflate the balloon by poking it with a needle. She said the inflated balloon was causing all of Joey's pain. I was about to ask for a sterile needle when Dr. Regina arrived.

Dr. Regina spoke to Beth briefly on my phone. She asked the ultrasound technician for a sodium chloride flush. She emptied the flush and hooked the syringe to Joey's G-tube. Gently, she pulled on the plunger and water entered the syringe causing the balloon to deflate.

After deflating the balloon to half its size, she slid the balloon back into Joey's stomach. Then, she used a sterile syringe of sodium chloride to fill the balloon up again. The trauma had created a gap around Joey's G-tube through which the stomach's contents continued to leak.

I covered the area around the tube with gauze and a towel but the leakage was relentless. Joey had reached his limit and found himself reduced to tears. I held his hand and Alicia told him she loved him. We told him we were sorry all this was happening to him. Dr. Regina comforted Joey as well. She told him he was a strong young man. Then she instructed the nurse to give him a pain bolus.

After everything calmed down, Joey was told the ultrasound had to be completed. Can you imagine looking down and seeing half a balloon protruding through your skin from your stomach and your stomach contents leaking out all over you? Then, just minutes after pushing the balloon back into your stomach you have a technician doing an ultrasound on this tender area with fluids still leaking out? The pressure of the technician pushing down on the G-tube site was very discomforting, along with the mental trauma. Thank God for the pain bolus.

The ultrasound took longer than usual because the radiologist wanted to make sure Joey's stomach wall was stretched from the trauma and not torn. She also wanted to verify the G-tube's placement. Thankfully, his stomach had not torn and the tube placement came out well.

Leakage Battles

I found myself doing leakage control from this point on. I knew the stomach acid would make Joey's skin red and sore if I allowed his skin to be exposed to it. I washed the area after every leakage but I was having trouble keeping up. I called Beth to get advice. She suggested a colostomy bag and wafer. The contents would leak into the bag as the wafer protected the skin. I paged Joey's nurse and asked if she could get me a colostomy bag and wafer. She recommended the use of DuoDerm pads with the suggested setup.

I washed the area around the G-tube with warm water and dried it with a clean towel. I had to work quickly because the gap around his tube would leak on and off like a volcanic eruption. I placed

Nystatin powder on the area to prevent the growth of yeast and then patted the area with skin barrier. I cut a hole in the center of the DuoDerm pad and placed the pad around the G-tube. Then, I fitted the adhesive wafer over the pad to his skin at the tube site. The nursing assistant found a colostomy bag with an additional attachment at the bottom of the bag so it could be hooked up to Joey's drainage tube. The system seemed to work. The leakage ran into the bag and his skin was protected.

Now that Joey's wound was stable, I focused on his emotional state. The trauma of the protruding balloon was enough, but now the leakage was bringing back memories of his ileostomy days. He would sit and stare at the colostomy bag continually checking it for leaks. He would push the contents from the bag into the attached drain tube. I kept telling him to ignore the bag, but he just couldn't.

Poor Joey. Just a few days prior to all of this he was walking all over the place. Now, he was sitting in a chair afraid to move because his bag may leak. His quality of life had taken another hit.

Scared of Going Home

As our time to depart Texas grew closer, I felt a lot of anxiety and sadness. I was scared of going home because I was afraid of what lay ahead. We always hoped we would be traveling home from Texas with Joey in remission. The road we were traveling now was not the one we had prayed for. Our son was coming home because he wanted to spend time with his family and friends before his life came to an end. My heart ached when I thought of him seeing his home for the first time in months – knowing he was coming home to spend his final days there.

I could only imagine the thoughts he would be having. I knew I would cry for him the day we arrived home. What a bittersweet moment it would be for us. How would we deal with all the emotion? I missed home, but I knew I would miss my Joey even more. Alicia and Joey had made our house a home. Our home held so many precious memories... and now it would hold the memory of Joey's passing.

Packing is a Project

Sunday afternoon, before our scheduled departure from Texas, we cleared out the apartment. The weather outside was unbearably humid with a temperature of 104. Thankfully, the apartment was air-conditioned. We shipped thirteen boxes of Lego sets, disposed of ten bags of garbage, and gave away five bags of groceries. I took a long look around the apartment as sadness overcame me. Now, I had to face the reality of bringing Joey home.

EAT UP While You Can

Joey was eating like a trooper twenty-four hours after his G-tube incident. He said, "I might as well eat what I can, while I still can." He ate vanilla ice cream, spaghetti, grilled cheese, and pizza. I was concerned some of the foods may plug his tube, so I kept an eye on him as best I could.

Palliative Care Doctor Lays It on the Line

The day before our departure to Pittsburgh, another doctor from the palliative pain team stopped by to see Joey. She asked him about his pain and how he felt about leaving MD Anderson. Joey said, "My pain is a six out of ten, the G-tube leakage is stressing me out, and I'm not getting much sleep because of it. I'm feeling anxious about leaving, but I know it's time to head back home."

She asked him what he thought of future chemo treatments. He told her he wasn't sure what future chemo treatment, if any, he would have. He said, "I'll speak to Dr. Maurer in Pittsburgh about my pain and chemo options." Then he asked, "What will happen to me if my partial blockage becomes a complete blockage?"

She replied, "You would have to eat a lot softer foods and drink more liquids because everything would have to pass through your G-tube into the drainage bag. Your bowel would not turn necrotic because you would still be getting some blood supply to your intestines." She told him the tumor was big enough now that it was taking the nutrients from his body. Even though he was on TPN for food, his body was absorbing very little nutrients. She knew this because his Prealbumin level was low.

As she shared this information with Joey, my heart skipped a beat. Her statement made me realize my son was starting to starve as the cancer used him as a host. She said, "At some point, Joey, you will have to decide if the chemo treatments are more harmful to your life expectancy than doing nothing. Also, you will have to decide when to stop your TPN. When a person is in the dying process, the appetite decreases for a reason. The body doesn't want excess fluid because the fluid will leak out of the tissues into the body cavity causing pneumonia.

In other words, the TPN will start to fill your lungs and you will suffer from the very liquid that was being used to help you." I knew the day he stopped his TPN I would be a basket case, but I understood why he would have to do it.

At the end of her conversation, she told Joey he was a strong young man and she was glad to have met him. He thanked her for her time and sincerity. After she left, he asked us for a few moments to himself. Joe left the room ahead of me. I didn't follow him because I knew he needed some time alone. I stood in the hallway trying to process all we had been told. Joe returned a few minutes later. I gave him a hug and told him we would get through this together, one day at a time.

Acceptance

Later that night, Joe and I drove back to the apartment to turn in our keys. We didn't talk on the way because we were both taking in the reality that we were going to lose our son. Instead, we held each other's hand.

As soon as we entered the apartment, I started to cry. I told Joe I was going to miss Joey terribly and I couldn't imagine my life without him. I never thought the day would come when Joey wouldn't be with Alicia. I had always thought he would be playing with her children one day. I couldn't fathom talking to others about him in the past tense, including my future grandchildren. My heart hurt when I thought of myself saying, "Your Uncle Joey loved grilled cheese."

Joe told me he couldn't imagine life without Joey either, but we would have to accept it. We needed to stay strong for Alicia. She would need us more than ever when she lost her brother. I agreed. I knew I couldn't allow myself to be lost in grief when the time came for my Joey to leave us. Still, I knew I had to grieve at some point and I would need time to adjust to his loss. We mindlessly turned in the keys and I took one final look around the neighborhood as we drove back to the hospital.

Joey Has God On His Side

Several times Joey told me he had God on his side. He told me the Lord was with him and had always been with him. His transformation amazed and delighted me. A year ago my son was distant from God and now he craved to be near him, so much so he would pray daily in the hospital chapel and receive communion whenever a church representative came to visit. He read the Bible nightly, attended weekday and weekend masses, and began to ask me questions about my faith. I could see a visible change in him and I knew this difficult journey had led my son back to Jesus.

Knowing Joey had such love for God made my thoughts of losing him a bit easier to accept. He told me he would be in a better place waiting for us to join him. I knew one thing for certain...I wasn't scared of dying anymore. I knew I would be looking forward to seeing my son when my time came. Joey said, "I will come to meet you Mom, when it's your time. If I am allowed to." To see him again will be the happiest day of my life.

Joey was a true testament to the power of faith and its ability to sustain a person when all odds are against them. He continued to amaze and baffle those around him with his loving personality and determination. Against all odds, he walked on his own, built Lego sets, engaged others in conversation despite his high dosages of pain medication, and smiled often. No one could explain how he was able to do these things. Everyone admired him.

Returning to Pitt

The day before Joey's scheduled discharge, I received a phone call from Dr. Bartlett's assistant. She told me he had reviewed Joey's CT scan and agreed with the recommendation of the surgeon at MD Anderson. She told me she was sorry. I thanked her for the information and told her Joey's plans for returning home. I reported the news to Joey. He looked deeply troubled as he pondered his battle coming to its end.

Joey was discharged at 8AM on July 3, 2013. Thankfully, only a few doctors and nurses were there to see us off. Otherwise, the moment would have been too emotional. The nurse made sure we had all of our paperwork and medications. We were given pain medication for Linda to administer and enough TPN in freezer bags to last six days. We took a final look around the room as Joey settled himself into a wheelchair.

As we walked down the hallway towards the elevator, we fell silent. When we first arrived six months ago, we were filled with optimism and hope. Now, we were filled with melancholy and despair. We had hoped to leave here in remission, not waving a white flag in surrender.

We transferred Joey to our car and began our drive to Hobby Airport, about twenty-five miles south of Houston. We encountered very little traffic heading out of the city and made great time to the Wilson Air Center.

As soon as we arrived, we were told our plane was touching down. Joey was worried about his G-tube leaking during the flight. Of course, this anxiety lead to increased abdominal pain. As soon as the jet taxied in, Joey asked if Linda could give him a pain bolus. The plane came to a full stop and Linda hurried over to see us. She gave Joey a big hug. I told her he was in a lot of pain and she checked when his last dose had been administered. She was clear to give him a bolus.

The flight to Pittsburgh was pleasant. Joey enjoyed the take off and loved the view at altitude. About an hour into the flight, the G-tube started to leak. We brought towels along, so we placed one on his lap and another around the G-tube. Linda took good care of Joey throughout the flight. She monitored his pain and the leakage.

Two hours and fifteen minutes later, we landed in Pittsburgh. After exiting the plane, the pilots asked how Joey was doing. I told them he was heading home to spend his final days with us. The pilots went inside and came out with corporate tee shirts. As a keepsake, we had our picture taken outside the jet with them.

Joey thanked each of them for making his trip to and from Texas so memorable. Just before getting into the rental car, he gave Linda one last hug.

Children's Hospital of Pittsburgh UPMC

We arrived at the Children's Hospital and put Joey in a wheelchair to check in. We were told to report to floor nine. As soon as we arrived on the floor, we were escorted to the oncology clinic. Here, the nurses took Joey's vitals and led us to an exam room.

Dr. Maurer entered the room along with his team. He introduced himself and his two colleagues. After the proper introductions, he asked Joey to explain everything that had happened to him since he was first diagnosed with cancer. Joey told him all he knew.

He asked Joey what was going on with his pain and with his G-tube. Joey told him about the pain issues he was having and the incident that happened with his G-tube. Dr. Maurer asked what Joey hoped to accomplish for his future care. Joey told him he wanted to get as pain free as possible and he wanted to have some more chemo – if the treatment would extend his life with quality. Dr. Maurer explained to Joey his body had been through a lot of trauma already and his immune system was tired. He told Joey the wound area around his G-tube would be of concern to him for proper healing and potential infection. However, with that said, he would support Joey in whatever choice he made.

He told Joey he essentially had two choices. One choice was to skip chemo and return home on Palliative Care and Hospice. He assured Joey he would oversee his pain and he wouldn't be forgotten just because he wasn't in Pittsburgh. His second choice would be to undergo a cycle of Iranatecan and see how he tolerated it. He told Joey he felt the Iranatecan wouldn't provide him with a significant amount of extra time.

He asked Joey how much time he thought the chemo would give him. Joey said he was hoping for another six months to a year. Dr. Maurer told him he was sorry but he was most likely looking at a few months. Joey took the news hard. His eyes filled up and his expression became somber. I thought I was prepared to hear the news, but I wasn't. My heart felt like it had been pierced. His father was taking the news hard as well. After all, knowing something is one thing and hearing it is another. No matter how much you try, it's hard to accept. Dr. Maurer was very compassionate as he laid out his plan for Joey.

He would admit him to the hospital for two days. During those days, Joey would be placed on a PCA of Dilaudid and his G-tube would be changed over to a larger size to help stabilize the leakage. After that, he would discuss a possible cycle of Iranatecan.

Dealing with Death

After Joey was admitted to Children's Hospital, I found myself too tired to think. His room had a couch that converted into a bed. I set the bed up and fell asleep.

At 2AM, I woke up and found Joey staring at his father and me. He said, "I'm making memories." I knew he was thinking about his death and leaving all of us behind. He was scared of where he would go after he died, even though he believed in Heaven. He had so much on his mind and there was nothing I could do to help him. I said, "I'm making memories, too."

As he was coming to grips with his mortality, so was I. I didn't know if I wanted him to have chemo now because I didn't want him to get an infection and suffer. To me, he had suffered enough. At the same time, I wanted as much quality time with him as possible. I found myself praying for what was best for Joey instead of a miracle. I realized finding a cure wasn't an option anymore. I had given up hoping for it in Texas. Instead, I prayed for his peaceful passing and the strength to endure the loss of my son.

JULY-4th

Last July 4th we were in Pittsburgh waiting to see Dr. Bartlett for Joey's reversal surgery consultation. I had watched the fireworks from our hotel window. Now, I watched the fireworks from Joey's room in Children's Hospital. The sky above Three Rivers Stadium was ablaze with colors but I found no joy in the festive display. Instead, I felt detached from the world. Lost in thought.

I felt like my son's life was being reflected back at me in the night sky...bright and colorful explosions that slowly faded away as their light extinguished. Why did my son's bright, shimmering light have to be extinguished? I looked out the window and said, "Maybe it's because the best firework to see is usually the one that is the brightest and the shortest lasting of them all."

The Shower

On July 5th, a surgeon came to remove Joey's G-tube and check the damage done to the site. She took a syringe and removed water from the G-tube balloon. Then, she gently pulled the tube out. Right away, she could see how big the hole had become. She told us she was going to leave the site open for the next few days so the skin could shrink and start to heal.

Shortly thereafter, a wound nurse came in and told us she recommended treating the area like an ostomy. She cleaned the skin and found a ring of yeast growing where the tube had been. The area was leaking so much stomach contents, the wound nurse had to use three towels to contain the liquid. She recommended Joey take a shower before she prepared the area for an ostomy wafer and bag. She asked Joey if he preferred me to help him with his shower or her. He said, "I prefer my Mom."

The moment I helped him undress, my heart broke. I knew he was thin, but the cancer was wasting him away. He looked like a concentration camp survivor. His skin hung from his bones and a sore was starting to form from pressure on his tailbone. His calves and feet were swollen making it hard to walk. He hunched over from abdominal pain and his eyes were dark and sunken. Why had he suffered so? Why was he reduced to this condition at such a young age?

Now, I understood why he preferred a sponge bath instead of a shower. If he took a shower he would have to see what this disease was doing to him. Seeing himself was too frightening. Standing in front of me was a vivid depiction of how destructive this disease had been to Joey's body, but not to his mind or spirit.

The Fever

At first, it was a real challenge to keep the wafer dry so it wouldn't have to be replaced every few hours. The combination of deep scarring and emaciation interfered with the wafer sticking properly to Joey's abdomen. We tried several different types and styles of wafers until we developed a system that worked. After that, Joey ate and drank what he felt his stomach could handle.

Once Dr. Maurer decided Joey's pain was under control, and his G-tube was stable, he told us Joey was ready for discharge. We left the hospital on a continuous PCA of Dilaudid and a continuous PCA of Versid. I was given emergency contact numbers in case Joey had any issues with pain. We arrived at our hotel shortly after 6PM. Joey was happy to be out of the hospital and eager to sleep in a regular bed.

Later that evening, a palliative nurse stopped by. She wanted to make sure Joey had all of his medical supplies. We went to bed right after she left.

Early the next morning, I took Joey's temperature. The thermometer read 99.9 degrees Fahrenheit. I called the emergency contact number for advice. I was told Joey would have to be brought to the Children's Hospital ER if he spiked a fever of 101 or higher. At 7PM, Joey had a temperature of 102. Poor Joey, he couldn't catch a break.

At the ER, Joey was placed in an isolation room. Cultures were taken from his PICC line and peripheral blood. He also had a chest x-ray. After six hours in the ER, he was admitted to the oncology floor, so much for Joey's wish of sleeping in a regular bed.

Dr. Maurer came to see us at 9AM. He told Joey his cultures were negative but he felt his body wouldn't be able to handle further chemo. He told Joey if he gave him chemo he would shorten his life. Joey took the news with grace and poise. He asked Dr. Maurer what his recommendation would be. Dr. Maurer told Joey he would send him home under Palliative Care & Hospice and he would remain his primary physician.

I felt my heart sink and my hopes deflate when Joey was told the news. I knew Joey was too weak to handle any more chemo. I just hated knowing he had to lose this battle after he had fought so hard for so long. I wasn't mad at God, but I was disappointed. Joey had so many people praying for him over the past months. I was told there were people praying for him that had left the church. In Joey, they had found a renewed sense of purpose. Why did their prayers have to be answered like this?

Joey told me he felt sad and scared by the news his treatments were finished. However, he was glad Dr. Maurer had made the decision for him because he never wanted to be called a quitter. I told him no one would think of him as a quitter. He was a fighter. He had put up one hell of a fight over the past sixteen months. Despite all the pain and suffering, he had managed to stay positive in attitude, strong in faith, and consistent in acceptance of God's will. I, like so many others, was humbled by his ability to go through all that he had. I said, "Joey, you just didn't speak of your faith – you lived it."

8

Coming Home to Say Good-Bye

"While I thought that I was learning how to live, I have been learning how to die." — ***Leonardo Da Vinci***

Dr. Maurer's team set up Hospice for us. A hospital bed, wheelchair, shower chair, and suction machine were delivered to our home. Their delivery was coordinated with Alicia. Joey wanted the hospital bed set up in the living room next to the fireplace where we put the Christmas tree during the holidays. He wanted the bed there so he could see everyone easily and be involved in family and visitor interactions, rather than being isolated in a bedroom.

Joey was discharged on July 9th. We left the hospital at noon. I drove with Joey in the front seat next to me. He placed a towel over his lap and one across the seat underneath him in case his G-tube leaked. Joe rode in back.

Part of me was happy to be going home. The other part of me was filled with sadness and depression. I still couldn't believe we were bringing our son home to die. I knew passing away at home, surrounded by his family, was Joey's wish. So, it was our desire and obligation to fulfill it. Clinging to that thought gave me some comfort.

The drive seemed endless despite the absence of roadwork. Once, Joe yelled at me for watching Joey instead of the road. I veered to the right and the tires hit the grooved asphalt causing the steering wheel to vibrate. Thinking it was time to let Joe drive, I pulled over at the next rest area. Joe got himself a hamburger, Joey a milkshake, and I opted for nothing. My stomach couldn't tolerate a thing.

When we were back on the road, Joe made a comment I took the wrong way. Thinking back, I know I was overtired because I can't even remember what his comment was. Joey told us to stop bickering. He said he sensed a lot of anger in the car and he felt we were mad because we were going home for him to die.

He was right. He told us to say out loud, "This is not my fault." So, all three of us said the phrase out loud three times. Saying the phrase helped. Again, Joey had demonstrated his ability to see beyond himself.

Alicia and Brandon were waiting for us when we arrived home. As we entered the house, Joey's eyes fell on the hospital bed by the fireplace. He sighed and said, "So this is where it will happen." There was very little any of us could say in response. I touched his shoulder and told him I was sorry. He gave me a hug as we held back tears. We were home and I wanted so badly to be back in Texas.

The fact our son was going to pass away in our living room was heartbreaking for me. A room where he took his first steps as a baby, opened his Christmas presents, and searched for Easter eggs. A room where he and his friends played hours of video games, where he had wedding pictures taken with his sister, and where he shared countless hours of movies with his father and me. How could this be possible? We had brought our Joey home to say goodbye.

Meeting the Hospice Team

After we got all the medical supplies and suitcases in the house, we unpacked the necessities. We ate a light dinner, visited for a while, and went to bed early. Joe and I slept on each end of our large sectional couch and Joey slept in his hospital bed next to us. By using his favorite pillows and blankets from his bedroom, Alicia made his bed as comfortable as possible. Next to him, on the fireplace hearth, I placed a large plastic container full of his medical supplies along with an IV pole to hang his TPN. I hooked Joey up to his nightly TPN and told him I loved him.

Early the next morning, Joey's Hospice nurses arrived. After Ed and Kate were introduced, we sat down and filled out the necessary paperwork. Ed gave Joey a physical, verified all his medications, and transferred over his PCA pumps. Joey was on a continuous dose of Dilaudid with a bolus every 10 minutes, along with a continuous dose of Versid.

Ed heard some gurgling sounds in Joey's left lung, so Joey's TPN was reduced to prevent fluid buildup. I was scared because I knew this was the first step in getting Joey ready to pass comfortably. We had been home less than a day and the preparations had already begun.

The Hospice team provided me with a booklet to review. Ed suggested a few specific pages for me to read. He asked me to post Joey's DNR orders on the refrigerator and to keep a copy of his Living Will/Health Care Proxy close by. The whole assessment, with introductions, took about two hours. Prior to departing, Ed told Joey he would be back to check on him in the morning.

Dr. Maurer Achieves Cooperation

Dr. Maurer called shortly after the Hospice team left. He told me the Hospice here had considered removing him as Joey's physician because he was in Pittsburgh; however, he had spoken to the local Hospice primary physician and he had agreed to cooperative care. The local physician would be Joey's primary doctor and he would be advised by Dr. Maurer.

At this point, Joey's liver was healthy and tolerating the high level of pain medications. The local Hospice doctor wasn't knowledgeable about the specialty of Joey's situation and Dr. Maurer explained its depth to him. The Hospice nurses expected to see Joey incoherent and bedridden on the Dilaudid. They were amazed to find him alert and greeting them at the front door when they arrived. He even told them his social security number.

I was happy the doctor here was willing to work with Dr. Maurer on Joey's pain care. Taking Joey all the way back to Pittsburgh would have been difficult, but I would have done it to keep Dr. Maurer involved. I had promised Joey he would have Dr. Maurer and I would keep that promise to the best of my ability.

Joey Prepares for His Passing

Later that day, Joey took time to tell each one of us how much he loved us and would miss us. He met with each of his cousins and best friends privately, and offered each one some personal item to remember him by. Each item had a specific meaning to him.

My heart hurt, though I hid my emotions, as he opened a tiny cedar chest and withdrew treasures, telling me to whom he would give each one. He gave his watch to his best friend Michael. Michael had originally broken it when they were clowning around several years ago on a trampoline. Since that time, Joey had gotten the watch fixed. He also gave Michael a Samurai sword, and his new leather coat from Christmas. He lovingly offered his cousin James his two favorite necklaces. He gave his best friend Kyle his favorite silver rope bracelet, along with a few swords from his collection. To his cousin John he gave a German World War II dagger they had both gone to purchase at an antique show when Joey was twelve years old. He gave Brandon his Remington shot gun, his Bible, and his telescope. He gave his childhood girlfriend, Marissa, his black wool coat that he wore when they went Christmas shopping together the Christmas before he was diagnosed. He gave his Aunt Tari his silver ID bracelet.

He gave Alicia his childhood Baby Bunny, his dog tags, his class ring, his Army uniforms, and his National Guard St. Christopher necklace. He gave his father and me his new Ford Escape, which he had driven only a few times since his cancer diagnosis, along with the pick of any other items we wished to keep. Naturally, we told him we would display all of his Lego sets. One morning, he handed me a zip lock bag full of letters and small notebooks. He told me he wanted me to read them so I would get to know him better when he was gone. I promised him I would.

On the days he felt decent, we would go for a short walk up and down our road. I would push Joey in his wheelchair and Alicia would walk beside us. On one such occasion, his cousin James pushed him in his wheelchair. Joey really enjoyed that. He would talk as we walked, but never about himself. Instead, he would spend his time cracking jokes or making faces to make all of us laugh. He never felt outwardly sorry for himself. I guess I felt enough of that for both of us.

I felt sorry for him every moment of every day. As we walked, I would think to myself how sad it was to know this summer would be his last. The last time he felt the sunlight on his face or the warmth of a summer breeze against his cheeks. How it hurt me to think this would be the last summer I would walk beside my son listening to the birds singing as he pointed out the flowers. It hurt too deep for words and too intense for comfort. I had all I could do to contain my emotions in front of him...to seem untouched by the reality of it all.

Moments like these made me realize my son was dying and so was I. I was experiencing a slow emotional death with each passing day. As his strength slowly faded and his bright brown eyes dimmed, so did mine in perfect unison. The only difference was his was occurring outwardly on the surface for all to see and mine was buried deep inside.

Planning for Kyle's Wedding

Joey wanted to be in Kyle and Rachel's wedding on August 3rd. We took him for his tuxedo fitting on July 12th. The day of the fitting Joey had all he could do to get up and get into his wheelchair, but he did it.

The woman measuring him was noticeably touched by his determination and, simultaneously, overwhelmed by his frailty. She tried her best to hide her pity as she measured him. But, I think she almost lost it when he said, "Can I look at brown tuxes? I would like one for my funeral."

Leave it to Joey. He selected a traditional tuxedo in chocolate brown with a light beige textured vest and tie. He also picked out a pair of new black shoes. Not too many people could do such a thing, but Joey was not your typical person. We all had come to know this by now. It took every ounce of my being not to cry as he showed me the tuxedo.

The drive to and from the tuxedo shop took its toll on Joey. He was exhausted by the time we got home, but he had accomplished what he had set out to do.

Joey Picks His Memorial Stone

Joey asked me to help him pick out his memorial stone. I spent hours looking through pictures. I finally came across a statue of St. Michael the Archangel. In the statue design, Michael was a young man holding his sword down to the ground in his right hand and holding his left hand, palm up, as his head looked towards Heaven. He wore armor similar to a Roman soldier, minus the helmet, and his wings folded behind him towards the ground. Both St. Michael and Joey fought battles against evil. St. Michael fought against the devil and Joey against the evil of cancer. This memorial statue was perfect. Joey loved it.

I contacted a local monument dealer and set up an appointment to meet with her. When she came to the house we showed her the picture of the statue. She discussed the design and size with us and showed us samples of granite. Joey remained in his bed as I reviewed the details with her. After I had the details down, I presented them to Joey. He gave his input, changes were made, and a final design was agreed upon.

The end result would be a statue made from gray granite standing four feet tall, eighteen inches thick, and two feet wide. The statue would be mounted on top of a four feet long, ten- inch high slab of polished blue granite. This slab would have the following verse engraved in it:

Hush My Dear Son Lie Still In Slumber, Holy Angel Guard Thy Bed
Heavenly Blessings Without Number, Gently Fall Upon Thy Head

The engraved polished blue granite slab would sit on top of a six feet long, ten-inch high slab of rough gray granite.

The Grave Site

On July 18th, all of us drove to St. Peter's Cemetery. It was a very hot day and Joey wasn't feeling the best. We decided he should remain in the air-conditioned car with Brandon and Alicia while Joe and I met with the caretaker in the cemetery office.

The caretaker walked us outside and showed us the available areas. We had Brandon drive the car to the different areas so Joey could see them. Joey selected an area about fifteen feet off the main road in an open portion of the cemetery. His statue would sit nicely here by a big Oak tree. Joey asked everyone if they liked the spot. We all agreed the location was nice.

We decided Joey's memorial stone would be our family stone as well. We told him his statue would be set up as he designed, however, we would add the name "CHUBBUCK", in big letters, above the verse. Joey liked the idea. Joey amazed us all that day with his strength and courage as he picked out his final resting place.

Missing in Action

One afternoon, Joe saw a military man getting out of his car in our driveway. He thought he might have heard about Joey coming home on Hospice and wanted to share the military's respects. Jokingly, Joey said, "No dad, he's here to take me away for failure to report."

The officer knocked on the door and I answered. He asked if Joseph M. Chubbuck lived at this address. I said, "Yes." He asked if he could speak with Joseph. He said, "I have papers indicating he failed to report to duty as assigned." I couldn't believe my ears.

I invited him in and pointed at Joey lying in his hospital bed. One look at Joey and the officer knew he was in an awkward situation. He asked Joey if he was Joseph M. Chubbuck. Joey said, "Yes Sir, I am." I spoke up and said, "He is terminally ill and has been honorably discharged since May."

He asked to see Joey's discharge papers. Joe got them. After reading the papers, he apologized to Joey and to us. He told Joey he hadn't received the paperwork and asked us to forward a copy to his office. In my opinion, the Army National Guard should be ashamed.

Physical and Emotional Suffering

The days grew tougher on Joey. He would experience bouts of nausea where I would have to suction out his G-tube with a syringe. Some nights, I found him suctioning his own G-tube because he didn't want to be a burden to me.

I watched Joey with admiration as he endured his pain and suffering without the slightest hint of bitterness. He would always say please and thank you whenever he asked for anything, whether it be a glass of Kool-Aid or an ice pack for his back. He managed to maintain a sense of humor despite it all.

As I watched Joey slipping away, I found myself struggling with fear, grief, and acceptance. I prayed constantly to have the ability to accept God's will. I thought to myself, "Cancer must be pure evil as it destroys itself along with its host." I knew this disease couldn't be of God's doing. It was designed to turn man against God...to cause the afflicted and their loved ones to question their faith and to resent God. But my son hadn't allowed that to happen.

Instead, Joey inspired others by his daily actions and deeds. He encouraged people to pray, to care for others, and to bare their sufferings as part of God's plan.

The chronic wasting began to worsen. Joey's skin clung to his cheekbones and his eyes sank deeper within their sockets. Soon, dark shadows formed around them. He had little, if any, quality of life left. As his mother, I feared the loss of him, but at the same time I prayed for our Lord to take him and to end this torture. He deserved better than this. I found myself saying, "Please take him Lord, please, end his suffering."

Despite his cascading deterioration, every morning Joey would see me and say, "Good morning beautiful. How is the best mama in the world today?" I would smile and give him a kiss on his cheek and a gentle hug. I can't tell you how much I wished my hugs could take his pain away. He once said, "Your hugs feel good Mom. They make me feel better and a little safer, especially when I'm in pain or scared." So I hugged him as often as I could.

Nights got worse for Joey. He began to dread the pain, anxiety, and restlessness. We hated to see him in so much discomfort. Many times, I sat in bed next to him holding his hand as he laid his head on my shoulder. This seemed to comfort him and he was able to get some sleep.

One morning, after he woke up, he asked me if I was scared. I said, "I'm scared every day." He said, "Me too." I told him Jesus was scared of dying. The Bible spoke of it as his agony in the garden. I told him Jesus was human like him and he, too, was afraid of dying. Why else would he have cried and prayed to our Lord for the cup to pass him by? Joey said, "I never thought about that."

Joey then asked if how he was feeling now was how it felt to be dying. I asked him how he felt. He told me he felt strange and not right...blah feeling. He said he felt extremely tired and weaker with each passing day. Like he just wanted to close his eyes and go to sleep.

I held his hand and said, "Yes, Sweetheart, I believe you are in the process of dying. I think this is how death is going to feel to you because you are not getting enough nutrients. I'm sorry, Joey." He looked deep into my eyes and said, "I'm sorry I can't take your pain away, Mama." I wrapped my arms around him as the tears I had been holding back streamed down my cheeks.

I wanted so badly to take the cancer away so he could live. I said, "I wish I could trade places with you." He said, "I would never wish that on you or anyone else. I want you to live a long and full life...to have fun for at least another forty years." I replied, "Forty years without you would be far too long, I would miss you too much. I can't imagine my life without you." He put his arms around me, gently kissed me on the forehead, and whispered, "You'll have to."

He asked me to take care of Alicia, Brandon, and his Father. I promised him I would. He told me my faith would help me cope with his loss, but he was worried about them. Their faith wasn't as strong. Then, he said, "Do you believe in Heaven or something after death?" I said, "Yes, I believe in Heaven or a state of consciousness after death when one is with God." He said, "I'm afraid of dying Mom. What if nothing exists after death, even though I have faith that it does?"

I told him it was normal to have doubts and fear, to question the existence of Heaven. Especially when facing one's mortality, no matter how much faith one claims to have. I told him I would be scared when my time came, even though I believe in Heaven. I said, "Pray for strength Joey, strength to overcome fear and accept death as a gateway to a new life."

He looked at me with his big brown eyes saying, "I will miss you, Dad, and Alicia very much. I'm not ready to leave, but my body is shutting down on me." I said, "I will miss you too, Sunshine. But time in eternity will pass quickly and we will soon be there by your side. Like a happy dream that makes the night fly by in what seems to be a heartbeat." He gave me a soft smile and I promised him everything would be okay. We would miss him, but he shouldn't be afraid to let go. I said, "Go to the light or with your angel, Joey, if one comes for you. You deserve to be happy and healthy again." He said, "Don't forget me Mom." I said, "We will never forget you Joey. We love you too much."

Then, he said, "I have one wish if I make it to Heaven. I will ask Jesus to give Alicia a baby because I know how hard she had been trying for one." I replied, "I'm looking forward to your wish coming true."

Later that morning, Ed came to check on him. He told me Joey was in the process of dying and he would probably experience bouts of discomfort where he would complain of not being able to find a comfortable position in the bed or elsewhere. This is known as Terminal Restlessness. He told me to call Hospice if his discomfort or anxiety increased so his medications could be adjusted. He told Joey to call if he needed him.

Sister Rosaire & Father Hearn

Joey had graduated from Rome Catholic School in 2009, and Sister Rosaire had been the school librarian since Joey was a preschooler. She heard Joey was sick and remained in contact with us. After we returned home on July 9th, she and Father Hearn began to visit Joey. They usually came at separate times. Sister would stop by on Mondays to give Joey communion. Father came by later in the week. He would visit with Joey and give him spiritual comfort.

One particular day, Father came to Anoint Joey. Joey got out of bed, shaved, and put his best cloths on. He said, "Father Hearn doesn't need to see me looking bad." When Father arrived, Joey answered the door. Father was amazed to see him dressed up and greeting him. Joey invited Father in and offered him something to drink. Father couldn't get over Joey's concern for him despite his own condition. After the Anointing, he told Joey he was an amazing young man. Joey said, "I always feel better after seeing you, Father."

On Monday, July 22nd, I started to cry as Sister was praying with Joey. My heart was heavy because I knew Joey's time was drawing near. I was overcome with grief as I watched my precious child being tortured day in and day out while I stood by helplessly watching. Sister gave me a hug saying, "I will pray for Joey's peaceful release."

A few days later, Father stopped by with his seminarian. Joey enjoyed visiting with them. Before departing, Father told me he would be stopping by more often. He knew Joey's time was close at hand.

Memories in the Making

Alicia really wanted Joey to see all his Lego sets on display before he passed away. She asked us if she could remodel our study. We loved the idea. She painted the room beige and purchased two bookshelves to display Joey's Lego sets on. She printed and framed various photos of Joey, throughout his illness working on the Legos, and placed them throughout the room. With great care, she transformed the study in to a room dedicated to her brother.

After the study was completed, I asked Alicia to go through all the family photos and select pictures of Joey she could use on picture boards. I know this sounds harsh, but I knew the picture boards could be put together better now than after he had passed away. Alicia understood my request. She made three picture boards over the course of a week. Joey never knew about them.

As I watched her create the boards, I felt a deep sadness. She included pictures of Joey with each family member as well as his best friends and classmates. As I looked over the boards, I would flash back to the actual day of each picture as if it were happening in front of me. Where had the time gone? How could it have come to this... wonderful memories being placed on a poster board for my twenty-two year old son's soon-to-be funeral? My eyes welled up with tears as I gently ran my hand across the pictures of Joey and his sister – Halloween, Christmas, swimming in the pool, snowball fights, class pictures, proms, Alicia's wedding, and Joey's boot camp graduation – snapshots of a life ending too soon.

Mingled within these pictures were pictures of Joey and us throughout his illness – pictures of him building his Lego sets, sleeping with his head on my shoulder, walking with his Father, and getting coffee with Alicia. I wondered why this had to happen to Joey and to our family. I knew I would never understand.

9
Mama, It's Time

"Faith is not so much something we believe; faith is something we live." — ***Joseph B. Wirthlin***

As Joey's fatigue increased, so did his inability to find comfort in any position. The nights became longer and much more difficult on him. He would put a cold compress on the back of his neck, another on the top of his head, and one on each side of his lower back.

On Monday, July 29th, he asked me if I thought he could be in Kyle and Rachel's wedding on August 3rd. I said, "I'm sorry Joey, but I think you're too weak to be in the wedding." He said, "I thought so too. I've been trying to hang in there for the wedding. I hate to let Kyle and Rachel down. But I don't want to go to the wedding and be a distraction. I guess it's time for me to go Mom. So I can be at the wedding in spirit. Call Ed and tell him I want to increase my pain medication and discontinue my TPN."

I called Ed and he spoke to Joey's doctors. Joey's requests were approved. Ed came over and made the appropriate changes to Joey's pain pumps as I dumped the remaining bags of TPN down the sink. On the outside, I looked composed. Inside, I was a mess. I knew I had to get a grip on the harsh reality that, very soon, my son wouldn't be here.

Joe came home from work and we told him what Joey had decided. Ed told Joe that he had a long, sincere conversation with Joey and Joey knew his body was shutting down. Ed gave both of us a hug and told us to call him if we needed him. With tears in his eyes, he shook Joey's hand before leaving.

Joey was lying in bed when his Dad came in to give him a hug. Joey said, "Are you alright, Dad?" As he hugged Joey, Joe shook his head no and began to cry. Joey began to cry, too. Seeing them both crying made me cry. Joe said, "This just isn't fair. This shouldn't have happened to you at such a young age when you had so many dreams and plans ahead of you. I will never understand why this had to happen. I'm sorry I couldn't protect you Joey." Joey said, "This is not your fault, Dad. You did all you could do for me. I love you very much and you're a great father. It's all part of God's plan, Dad. A plan I don't understand now but I will once I pass away."

At this point, Alicia arrived home. She gave Joey a hug and held his hand. We decided to give them some private time together so they could say what needed to be said.

Terminal Restlessness

The lack of hydration began to take its toll on Joey, yet he remained alert and functional. He was determined to take care of himself. He asked his father and me for help to get up and walk to the bathroom. We were amazed by his will power. He put an arm around each of us and slowly walked to the bathroom despite his weakness. Joe helped him in and I waited until he was finished to help him return to his bed. When we told Ed what he had done, he couldn't fathom how Joey was able to function, let alone get up and walk, considering the state his body was in.

As the hours passed, Joey slept more and more and only woke up when he wanted to ask us for a cool drink or an ice pack. As he was sleeping, we would take turns making sure the ice packs were kept cool for him and positioned where he wanted them. I would change his G-tube dressing as needed, and rub his feet, legs, and arms with moisturizing lotion to prevent dryness and bedsores. As the evening settled in, all of us sensed that it wouldn't be long before we lost our Joey.

Brandon and Alicia had been staying with us since Joey's return from Texas. They wanted to spend as much time with Joey as possible. They went to bed around 10PM and Joe and I assumed our usual sleeping positions on either end of the couch.

By midnight, Joey's terminal restlessness peaked. His mind seemed to fog over and he lost all sense of reality. He took some of his clothing off and crawled out of bed. We would help him to the floor so he didn't fall or get hurt, but he wouldn't speak to us. He would just lay there curled up in a fetal position. I would cover him with a bed sheet. Our hearts broke watching him. He would sleep for twenty minutes or so, then he would get up on his forearms and knees and rock back and forth in an attempt to stand. Again, we would help him up and into his bed. In bed, he would turn from side to side. We tried to comfort him by telling him we were there and we loved him. We held his hand but sometimes he would push our hands away. This behavior went on for several hours. Just when we thought we couldn't take it any more, it stopped.

Joey's Passing

Joey was in and out of consciousness for the rest of the morning. His breathing was intermittent and shallow with slight pauses lasting ten seconds or longer. Joe sat by his side holding his left hand, Alicia held his right hand, and I placed my hand on the top of his head. Every so often I would rub the side of his face and whisper I love you. I don't know if he heard me but it made me feel better saying it to him.

For a moment he opened his eyes and looked at me. He whispered, "I'm sorry I can't take the pain from your eyes, Mama. I love you." I gently hugged him saying, "That's okay Sunshine, I love you too."

Outside, the sky was dark and overcast. Our dog, Ruckus, began to cry and whine with his tail tucked between his legs. He panted uncontrollably and refused to settle down. I went to him in an attempt to calm him. After this failed, I let him outside.

After returning to Joey's bedside, he made an attempt to sit himself up but his neck was too weak. His head bobbled and dropped from side to side and back and forth like a newborn baby's. His eyes opened and closed. Suddenly, he slapped himself across the face as hard as he could twice in a row. He shook his head as I grabbed his hand saying, "Don't do that Joey. You are home. Alicia, Dad, Brandon, and I are with you. You are safe sweetheart. It's okay." For a brief second, he acted as if he was trying to locate my voice. Then, he gently laid his head back on the pillow and closed his eyes. His body relaxed and his breathing stabilized.

He remained this way for quite some time, so I decided to take a seat next to him on the couch. Alicia sat next to me and Brandon sat at the far end of the sofa. Joe continued to kneel by Joey's side holding his hand. Since Joey's condition appeared to be stabilized, Joe decided to make himself something to eat. He let go of Joey's hand, kissed him on the forehead, and said, "I love you, Joey."

A few minutes later, Joey let out a sigh. At first I didn't give it much thought as he had made similar sounds in the past. Suddenly, a strange feeling overcame me. I looked over at Joey. I glanced at his chest and saw no movement. His bed was slightly reclined so he was sitting in a semi-upright position. His head hung down and tilted slightly to the right. His eyes were half shut. I jumped to my feet saying, "I think Joey's gone." I ran to his side, lifted his shirt, and placed my ear against his chest. No heartbeat. I picked up a nearby stethoscope and listened again. Nothing. I began to cry. The time was 3PM on Thursday, August 1, 2013. My precious little boy had passed. I said, "My Joey's gone."

My mind went blank as I put my arms around him. A tiny teardrop rested on each of his cheeks. I pulled him tight against me. I was devastated. Why wasn't I holding his hand when he passed? How could I have let this happen? I had never left his side since he was diagnosed. The thought of him passing away without me holding his hand broke my heart.

As I was hugging Joey, sunlight filled our living room right over his bed as if the Lord was letting me know Joey's soul was being welcomed home. Joey was finally at peace. The sunlight dissipated and the sky became overcast again.

Hospice had advised us to take as much time with Joey as we wanted before calling them. So, we did. Each of us took turns holding Joey and getting the chance to say our private goodbyes. As Joe sat with Joey, I made calls to his family and mine regarding Joey's passing. Everyone I spoke to began to cry as soon as they heard my voice. They knew Joey had passed.

The hardest phone calls I made were to his two best friends Mike and Kyle. Kyle walked right off his job and drove to our house. I found him standing on my front porch in a daze. As soon as he saw me he hugged me and began to cry. I tried to reassure him. I told him Joey passed peacefully. He asked if he could see him. I walked him into the foyer. Joey's bed was visible from there and he looked like he was sleeping. As soon as Kyle saw him, he couldn't go any closer, all he could do was hug me and cry.

Not soon after this, Rachel arrived. I met her at the front door and she began to sob. I told them Joey wanted to be at their wedding in spirit so he decided it was time to go. I told them he wanted them to enjoy their wedding day. They told me he would still be a part of their wedding because they loved him so much. I asked them to check on Michael because I knew he had taken the news hard.

I called Ed shortly before Kyle showed up so he and Kate arrived around 4PM. They confirmed Joey had passed and called the funeral director. I deflated the balloon holding Joey's G-tube in place and gently removed the tube. I wiped the area clean and placed a small bandage over the hole. I reached over and took Joey's St. Christopher medal off his neck and gave it to Alicia. I removed his cloth rosary, given to him in Texas by a Catholic volunteer, and placed it around my neck as a keepsake. I left the brown scapula on him. I prayed its blessing held true and Joey had been greeted by an angel or Our Lady upon his passing.

The funeral directors arrived and asked us to stop by the parlor Friday morning to set up the funeral arrangements. They offered us the option of leaving the room when they transferred Joey to the body bag and stretcher. I opted to stay with him. I brought him into this world and I was going to be with him when he was taken. I made sure they kept him wrapped in his favorite brown blanket as they transferred him.

As stretcher was wheeled to the open front door, I walked beside Joey. Just before Joey was to pass through, I bent down and kissed him on the forehead. I closed the door behind them and walked to the kitchen window. There, I watched my son's body being taken down the front sidewalk to the waiting hearse.

The emotion I felt was overwhelming. I'm sure Joe and Alicia felt the same way.

Father Hearn & the Seminarian Visit

That evening, the doorbell rang. I opened the door to find Father Hearn and the seminarian standing there. I invited them in. Father placed his hand in mine and told me he was sorry for my loss. I told him what had transpired since he had last visited. When I told him Joey passed at 3PM, he smiled and said, "He passed at the Lord's hour. He was a special young man. He is with our Lord in Heaven on this day."

Hearing those words was the reassurance I needed. After you lose a child, no matter how much faith you have, you begin to question it. I thanked them both for coming to see Joey during his illness, for blessing him, and for stopping by to check on us.

Funeral Arrangements

The next day I realized how much Joey had done for us by making his arrangements. I never had to wonder if I was doing what he wanted. Joey and I had written his obituary a few days before his passing. All I had to do was select the photo I wanted to include with it. I selected a picture of him with his Father at his boot camp graduation. I flashed back to the day I took the picture. Joey looked so happy and healthy. That day was one of the happiest and proudest days of our lives. We hadn't seen Joey in weeks and we were so happy to be with him. Who would have guessed this picture would be used in his obituary two years later? My heart sank. Why Lord? I asked myself repeatedly as I wiped the tears from my cheeks.

Alicia wrote a poem for Joey entitled, *Another Summer Morning.* She told me she wrote the poem while sitting next to Joey the day before he died. She wanted to read the poem at his funeral mass. I told her Joey would be honored.

Another Summer Morning

By Alicia Marie Fleming for My Brother

Another summer morning, beside my brother's bed
Sitting, waiting, wondering
Another summer morning where he looks at me lovingly, asking how I am
Another summer morning, he will tightly grip my hand
Another summer morning, wishing God would grant me with
The serenity to understand, I can't change the way it is
The courage to change the things I can,
The wisdom to know the difference
But above all, the fearlessness, my little brother exhibits
Another summer morning, his chest will heave and fall
A hitch, a gasp, a breath, his body so weak, so small
Another summer morning, I softly touch his hair
A kiss upon his forehead, many more sent through the air
Another summer morning, I watch him suffer so
But he makes not one complaint,
Just a request, to God, to go
Another summer morning, his sunken broken eyes will cry,
He worries for his loved ones, scared for us, for when he dies
He wants us to be happy, to celebrate the gift of life
He makes me promise to go on, to love, to exist, to fight
Another summer morning, his shaking hands will cup my cheeks
But this morning is not like all the others, it's drab, it's dark, it's bleak
It's another summer morning, where his brilliance starts to fade
A star whose light has grown so weak, but will never wane away
And as his soul is freed, as he is taken from this world
I can't help but think back to the days; a young blissful boy, a little girl
A brother and a sister, two siblings, the best of friends
A plan to grow up with one another, side by side, hand in hand
Another childhood summer morning, running in the yard
Two best friends growing old together,
Sure they'd never part

But here I sit, as years long pass, an unfair fight he fought
A young boy, my brother, my best friend, a divine young life now lost
The summer morning creeps through the shades, it trickles across your cheeks
And my heart is lost without you, my lips part, I cannot speak
Another summer morning, beside my brother's bed
I know that though the sheets are made, you watch from overhead
Another summer morning, I miss your winning ways
I know my heart will be broken, until the end of days
Another summer morning,
Another autumn day,
Another winter wonderland, spring is on its way
Another day gone and passed,
And time keeps moving on,
But nothing is the same in your absence
Nothing, and...
Suddenly, it's another summer morning, without you...
Sitting... waiting... wondering

Her poem was full of emotion and pain. As she read it, I could envision them running hand-in-hand in the yard laughing. How I missed my son and how she was missing her brother. All I could offer her was a hug.

Friday morning, we took Joey's tuxedo, shoes, and jewelry to the funeral parlor to make his arrangements. Joey wanted to have his Grandfather's bracelet on and he wanted his black rosary in his hands. The times for Joey's calling hours and funeral mass were established. All that remained was the selection of his casket. The director took us downstairs to a display room. He told us about each type of metal and wood casket. Then, he gave us time alone to decide.

Alicia started to walk towards the hallway saying, "I have to use the restroom." Her Father said, "Alicia, I would wait and ask the funeral director. I wouldn't just go open a door somewhere." She said, "Are you being serious?" He responded, "Yes, dead serious." At which point we all started laughing. We knew Joey would appreciate the humor in the situation. The director returned and Alicia was led back upstairs to a restroom.

After her return, we selected a beautiful wooden casket with the Last Supper displayed on one side and the Blessed Mother holding Jesus in her arms on each corner. We signed the paperwork and left.

The rest of the morning was spent making bereavement dinner plans and ordering flowers, but not without constant thoughts of

Joey. I kept asking the Lord to let me know he was safe with him in Heaven, free from pain and healthy again.

Kyle & Rachel's Wedding

The Saturday after Joey passed away was Kyle and Rachel's wedding day. Joey told me he would be there in spirit. He had asked me to attend the wedding, so I planned on being present for the ceremony. I knew I wouldn't be up to staying for the reception. Joe accompanied me. The wedding was held outdoors. The forecast called for rain but the skies were sunny and blue. Joey was on duty.

When we first arrived, many of the people didn't know what to say. Soon, however, a few people broke the ice. They said they were sorry for our loss. We acknowledged their condolences with composure.

Just as the wedding party was lining up to begin their precession down the aisle, Kyle's dad came over and gave us a hug. He told us Kyle and Rachel wanted to see us. He led us to Kyle. As soon as Kyle saw us he gave us a hug and began to cry. We told him how proud we were of him and how handsome he looked. I said, "Joey is here in spirit Kyle, just like he promised." Then, Kyle's dad walked us to the back of the procession to see Rachel. She looked stunning. She gave us a hug as she cried. Joe said, "You look beautiful" and I said, "Joey is here in spirit with you on your special day." She dried her eyes and said, "Our wedding day is dedicated to Joey."

We walked back to our seats and the wedding began. There were four ushers and four bridesmaids, including the Best Man and Maid of Honor. We watched the first two bridesmaids walk down the aisle arm-in-arm with their usher. Then, my heart skipped a beat and my eyes filled with tears. Kyle's sister was walking down the aisle carrying an eight by ten framed picture of Joey with a yellow boutonniere taped to it. When she got to the front, she placed the picture on a table facing the crowd. The table was positioned right where Joey would of stood, had he been there, between the other two ushers. The Maid of Honor proceeded down the aisle ahead of Rachel and her father. Rachel was presented to Kyle and the ceremony began.

The minister said, "Kyle and Rachel wanted everyone here to know they had wished their best friend, Joseph Michael Chubbuck, could have been with them today. But they know he is here in spirit." He briefly described the battle Joey had fought and his passing just two days before. He asked everyone to bow his or her head and pray for Joey's spirit and for his family. Then, he proceeded with the ceremony.

After Kyle kissed the bride, they came down the aisle and gave us a big hug. Michael, the Best Man, was close behind. As Michael hugged me, he said, "I love you guys and I miss Joey so much."

After the ceremony, one of the bridesmaids came over and told me she knew Joey was at the wedding. She said, "When Kyle kissed Rachel two plastic love birds fell off the trellis over their heads and landed between them on the hem of Rachel's dress." I said, 'That sounds like something Joey would do."

Mike hugs me

Kyle hugs Joe

We didn't stay for the reception but we were told Joey's picture was placed at the head table where he would have been seated. In honor of him, no one sat in his chair the entire night. Michael said every wedding photo they took had Joey's picture in it, even Kyle's family photo. I couldn't think of a better way for Joey's memory to be honored. The love and respect they showed Joey proved they loved him as much as he loved them.

Joey's Calling Hours

The Monday following the wedding was Joey's calling hours. How I dreaded them, but I remembered what we had said to each other back in January. If he could endure them for me, then I would endure them for him.

Immediate family and our closest friends arrived at the funeral parlor an hour before the calling hours were to begin. Joe and I were the first to enter the room followed by Alicia and Brandon. Surrounding Joey's casket were bouquets of flowers – far more than we expected. I tried to contain my emotion as Joe and I walked towards Joey. My heart sank when I first set eyes on him. I knelt down and placed one hand over his as I looked at his face. His hand was cold but I didn't care. I just wanted to touch him and let him know we would never forget him. I whispered, "I love you, Joey, and we will never forget you Sunshine."

At that instant, emotion overcame Joe. He stood up and walked away. I went to him as Alicia and Brandon came forward to pay their respects.

Looking around the room, all of it seemed surreal to me. I felt like I was in a bad dream and couldn't wake myself up. To help maintain my composure, I began to read the cards on the various floral arrangements. Joey had arrangements from all over...I counted over twenty-five. A true tribute to him for all the lives he had touched.

Soon, people began to trickle in and the director asked us to form a receiving line. The picture boards Alicia had made were set up so people in line could view them as they waited. She also set up a large bowl of Reese's Peanut Butter Cups on a table near Joey's casket. She placed a note next to the bowl explaining how Joey would buy candy for his nurses as a thank you for caring for him and asking everyone to take one in Joey's honor.

The line of people waiting to pay their respects seemed endless. The entire time, I held a stone pocket angel Joey gave me when we were in Texas. He had said, "I got you this angel, Mom, because I knew you'd like it."

Sister Rosaire was kind enough to end Joey's calling hours with a prayer. After which we were too emotionally charged to go home. Instead, we went to a nearby restaurant to discuss the calling hours, how much we missed Joey, and our dread of having to say our final goodbyes.

Last Respects

The morning of the funeral, we all woke up with anxiety over the upcoming day. My stomach was a mess. I wasn't sure how I was going to handle the day's proceedings. We drove to the parlor in silence.

Friends and family were already waiting in the parking lot when we arrived, but we didn't speak to any of them. We went directly inside.

Joe and I knelt down to pay our respects to Joey. I felt such a deep longing to have my son back, to see him smiling at me, and to hear him laughing again.

As protocol dictates, Joe and I took seats with Brandon and Alicia in the front row of the parlor. Mike and Kyle sat behind us. As family came in, they were escorted to seats in the parlor by the funeral director. Once everyone settled in, Father Hearn began the prayer service. After he concluded the service, the funeral director called individuals up to pay their final respects. This was difficult on all present because Joey meant so much to everyone there. Not one person walked away without crying – male or female, young or old. The pain was evident in all of their faces.

The parlor slowly emptied until we were down to our immediate family and Joey's pallbearers. The funeral director asked the pallbearers to pay their final respects. The first to do so were Joey's four cousins – David, George, John and Jamie. It was hard to watch since I had so many memories of them playing together when they were little. Joey was the youngest and the one they all protected. Next, came Joey's best friends – Michael, Kyle, and David. Again, the memories flooded through me. Joey, Mike, and Kyle had been the Three Musketeers since fifth grade. David had worked with Joey and was always asking him for advice. All of them had lost a brother in their hearts. The last pallbearer to pay his respects was Brandon. He stood and bowed his head in respect before joining the others in the lobby.

Alicia, Joe, and I made our way up to the casket. All three of us held hands as we knelt down. I heard a deep and painful sigh come from Joe. I was too numb to express my pain. I flashed back to March 11, 1991. The day I first set eyes on Joey and held his tiny newborn hand in mine. Now, on August 6, 2013, I would hold his hand and set my eyes on him for the last time in this world. My maternal loss was beyond words.

Deep down, I knew I wasn't alone...other mothers had walked down this road besides me. But, at that moment, it was happening to me. I reached over and held Joey's hand saying, "I love you Sunshine and I will see you when my time comes." I said a Hail Mary and whispered, "Eternal rest grant unto Joey O Lord, and let perpetual light shine upon his face." Tears ran down my cheek as I gently let go of his hand. Kissing my fingertips, I gently placed them upon his cheek.

Joe placed his hand on top of Joey's and whispered, "Goodbye, Bubba. I love you and miss you so much." We stood up and stepped back to give Alicia time alone with her brother. Through tears, she gave him a kiss and spoke her own private words. Slowly, she stood up and walked into my arms.

After a few moments, we composed ourselves and walked to our car. There, we watched as Joey's pallbearers carried his casket to the awaiting hearse.

The Funeral Mass & Interment

Joey had asked Scott, his elementary band teacher and family friend, to sing at his funeral. He told us he wouldn't be able to see us before the mass or he would have a hard time singing. Joey had selected four songs. I asked Scott to sing an additional song dedicated to Joey from me.

As we approached the church, the sheer number of cars told us his mass would be full. Yet another testament to the impact Joey had on so many. During communion Scott sang *I Walk With God* followed by my requested song, *Wind Beneath My Wings*. Since Joey had been diagnosed, any time I heard this song I would think of him. He truly was my hero and everything I wished I could be.

As the funeral's closing remarks, Alicia read her poem with Brandon standing beside her for moral support. The entire church, including the priests, was reduced to tears. Joey's funeral mass was beautiful, a true reflection of the wonderful young man he was. As the funeral procession exited the church, the sun shined brightly.

A long line of cars followed our precession to St. Peter's Cemetery. There, Father Hearn performed a final blessing. Though the sun was shining and the sky was blue, my world felt dark and gray.

The Compassionate Doctors

After Joey's passing, I received an email from Dr. Wells telling me he was sorry they couldn't have done more to help Joey at MD Anderson. He prayed we would shed less tears as the days passed.
The Palliative doctor sent a beautiful sympathy card. Dr. Regina posted the following message on Joey's funeral condolence page:

"Joey will be remembered as an extraordinary young man – blessed with intelligence, maturity beyond his years, and kindness. I will never forget his courage, his humility, and his interest in the welfare of

others...he always demonstrated compassion and concern for the young patients in the hospital. I admired his ability to distract himself building complex Lego structures – even when he was not feeling well...and working hard to build his strength even as the disease progressed. I am certain he is at the Lord's table, having fought a good fight, finished the race, and kept the faith. GOD BLESS!" Regina

Dr. Zinner called to offer his condolences and sent the following email:

Dear Barb Chubbuck and Family,

I was mentioning last night to my wife, who is a physician here, your son's story and that I had spoken with you. The 15-20 minutes he spent with individual family and friends over the last 3 weeks and the gifts he gave to remember him by, his photo with a boutonniere attached put up next to his companion maid of honor at his best friend's wedding...my wife was very moved, as was I. I will never forget the butterfingers and the chocolate candies. He was a heck of a nice guy and obviously a young man of great spirit with a family that loved him deeply. Though it was profoundly generous of him to have appreciated that there is great tragedy in those even younger with cancer, he too was just setting out in life. I was always struck by your strength for your son...unimaginable how hard this has been. Your son had no business having had this happen to him but under these awful circumstances, he knew he had great love. Some of our most effective therapy is for the rarest cancers. I certainly hope others will benefit from what we can learn from Joey's cancer. Doing so will be another way to honor him. My kindest regards and very best wishes in this very sad time, even as we can celebrate a great life.

Ralph Zinner, MD

Sadly, the pathologists were never able to identify Joey's tumor type. Genetic testing indicated it might be a brand new variant of clear cell sarcoma. I sent the following email to Joey's Texas pathologist:

Hello Doctor,

This is the last email I will write to you. I just want to thank you for testing my son's tumor and to ask that you continue to do research at MD Anderson on unknown tumors like my son's. Joseph fought a hard battle and passed away peacefully at home in Rome, NY with all of us

near him yesterday afternoon. He was an amazing young man and he was a blessing to have in our lives for twenty-two years. Joey hopes the samples he donated for research will help others in the future. Foundations Medicine analyzed his tumor and found it had a EWSR1-ATF1 mutation which is very rare.
Kindest Regards,
Barb Chubbuck & Family

I received the following response:

Hi, Ms. Chubbuck,
My condolences to you and your family, I do appreciate this follow-up. EWSR1-ATF1 is rare and is being found in different tumors; it is interesting though that the morphology and immunohistochemical profile does not fit what was described (so far) with these tumors. It is possible this represents a new tumor, which has not been previously recognized before or a very bizarre variant, which has not been recognized before. Again, my sincerest condolences.

10

Keeping the Faith

"Keep the faith. The most amazing things in life tend to happen right at the moment you're about to give up hope."

— Author Unknown

The day after Joey's funeral I woke up to a persistent voice in my head telling me over and over, "Go before they're gone." So, I got dressed and drove to Joey's grave. When I arrived, next to his name marker, was a fresh bouquet of flowers. No card was on them. I reached down and picked the bouquet up. At that precise moment, a song came on my car radio – *"Only the Good Die Young".* I smiled as I remembered what I had said to Joey in January. I looked up and thanked Joey for the sign.

Later that day, I spoke to Michael. He told me he had a scare the night before. He had shut the light off in his bedroom and he thought he saw a silhouette of someone standing in the corner of his room. He got scared, so he said, "If it's you Joey, this isn't funny." Odd he should tell me this because the nurse's aide, who Joey was fond of in Pittsburgh, texted Alicia that same night to tell her she had experienced an unbelievable event. She told Alicia she had to contact her to deliver a message.

She had been sleeping when she felt pressure on her chest. She opened her eyes to see a silhouette of a young man in the corner of her room. Then she heard a voice say, "Tell Sis I'm healthy again." The silhouette disappeared and she started to cry. She didn't know if it was a dream or if it was real, but she knew she had to tell Alicia.

Alicia told us about the incident. She said a few days earlier, while visiting Joey's grave, she told him she was worried about him. She was afraid he was somewhere alone and frightened. She told him she would only believe she was getting a sign from him if the sign came from someone outside of the family who was not expecting one. Now, this had happened.

Tears

The day Joey passed away, he had a tear on each of his cheeks. As a mother I prayed for his passing to be peaceful and pain free. So, despite the signs we had been given, his tears troubled me. I hated the thought of his final moments being filled with fear. I had an innate need to protect him.

One night, after visiting Joey's grave, I came across a poem by David Romano entitled *When Tomorrow Starts without Me*. I read the following verse and knew I had my answer:

But as I turned to walk away, a tear fell from my eye,
For all my life, I'd always thought I didn't want to die,
I had so much to live for and so much yet to do,
It seemed almost impossible, that I am leaving you.

Knowing how hard Joey had fought to live this made perfect sense to me. Joey hadn't shed tears of fear that day, but tears of sadness. Though it was time for him to go, he wished he could stay. He had so much yet to do.

Joey's Wish Comes True

While on Hospice Joey said, "If I make it to Heaven, I'm going to ask Jesus for a baby for Alicia." In late September, Alicia told me she hadn't been feeling well. I told her she should take a pregnancy test. She said, "What for? The test will just come out negative like all the others I've taken over the past two years."

I smiled saying, "I didn't think so." We went to the store and bought an EPT test. The test came back positive. Alicia was pregnant! Tears streamed down our faces as we realized Joey's wish had come true.

That evening, after Alicia had shared the news with Brandon, we all met at Joey's grave to surprise Joe. Alicia presented her Father with a baby tee shirt that said "Best Grandpa" on the front. At first, he didn't know what to make of it. Then, it hit him. He threw his arms around Alicia shouting, "You're pregnant!"

We asked Alicia if she wanted a boy or a girl. She said, "Joey knows I want a boy. I told him I would name my baby after him."

On May 13th, nine months and twelve days after Joey's passing, Alicia gave birth to a beautiful baby boy. She and Brandon named him Isaac Joseph Michael in memory of his Uncle Joe.

Isaac Joseph Michael

11

Strength Beyond Measure

"You have power over your mind – not outside events. Realize this, and you will find strength." — ***Marcus Aurelius***

Joey passed away a year and a half ago, and I still have vivid images of him and his ordeal. The whole experience had such a profound impact on me. I cannot begin to tell you how much I learned from my son during the course of his illness. I witnessed firsthand the tenacity of the human spirit, the power of love, and the strength of the human mind.

From the beginning, Joey possessed maturity beyond his years. He had the ability to accept the battle that lay before him, no matter the outcome. He faced each day with an inner strength and fortitude that I never thought was possible. No matter how hard the cancer hit him, he managed to take a shot back at it. He refused to let cancer control his life.

Just like Stuart Scott stated, "When you die, it does not mean that you lost to cancer. You beat cancer by how you live, why you live, and in the manner in which you live." Well, Joey made these words a reality for myself, and many others that knew him. Cancer didn't define Joey. His strength, determination, and resilient faith did.

Every evening, in the hospital, Joey would push his IV pole to the gift shop. There, he would buy candy bars for the nurses that took care of him that day. No matter how ill he was, to the amazement of many, he managed to do this. He would say, "This is the least I can do to thank them."

No matter how difficult things became, Joey managed to find some light in the darkness...some silver lining. Many of his nurses told me they went home with a different outlook on life after spending time with him. His Hospice nurse said, "Joey didn't teach me how to live. He taught me something far more important, he taught me how to die."

Joey set the bar so high that we no longer complain or feel sorry for ourselves. When life hits us hard, we just hit back using the hope, attitude, resilience, and determination Joey taught us.

As James Merritt said, "Real faith can stand the refining fire of suffering and undeserved evil and come out even stronger and more resilient." I believe Joey possessed this kind of faith. As his body succumbed to the suffering inflicted upon it by the evil of cancer, his faith and will strengthened.

Joseph Michael didn't lose to cancer, cancer lost to Joseph Michael. He never let cancer destroy his faith, his zest for life, or his loving nature. Like the soldier he was, Joseph looked fate in the eyes, battled cancer on his own terms, and faced death with strength beyond measure.

The author's proceeds from the sale of this book will be donated to

The Joseph Michael Chubbuck Foundation, Inc.

A Charitable Organization – contributions to which are tax-deductible

"Helping Cancer Patients & Their Families"

www.thejmcf.org

Works Cited

Merritt, James. God, I've Got A Question. Oregon: Harvest House Publishers, 2011. 92. Print.

www.ingramcontent.com/pod-product-compliance
Ingram Content Group UK Ltd.
Pitfield, Milton Keynes, MK11 3LW, UK
UKHW041824200726
13854UKWH00002BA/540